CARMEN / *No. 9 Seguidilla*

Close by the walls of Se - vil - - la,
Près des rem - parts de Sé - vil - - le,

ROBERT VAVRA

William Morrow & Company, Inc.

The Sevilla of CARMEN

With a commentary by James A. Michener

For Barbara, who like Bizet has never visited Sevilla but because of Carmen *has felt its passion*

Copyright © 1985 by Robert Vavra

Grateful acknowledgment is made to the following
for permission to use previously published materials:
Dover Publications, Inc.
Random House, Inc.
Riverrun Press, Inc.
Schirmer Books

(dust jacket photograph) The eyes of Rosario Sanchez, wife of a Sevillano matador

(title page photograph) This is Sevilla as seen from Triana. The cathedral appears in front of the rising sun on the left page and the Tower of Gold on the right page.

Library of Congress Catalog Card Number: 85-60714

ISBN 0-688-05880-9

Printed in Spain by Grafos, S. A.
P.º Carlos I, 157 - 08034 Barcelona
Depósito Legal B. 21004-1985

First Edition

4   1 2 3 4 5 6 7 8 9 10

CONTENTS

FOREWORD BY JAMES A. MICHENER

Sevilla I remember with special affection not only because of its romance and unique charm, or *gracia*, but because it was there that the idea was born for *Iberia*, a book that I have often said is a personal favorite among those that I have written.

In *Iberia* I commented: "If Córdoba is the apex of the Romantic Movement because of *Don Alvaro . . .*, Sevilla is the popular capital because of the works which have used this city as their locale. The story of *Carmen* takes place in Sevilla and one needs no imagination to see the gypsy lounging in the doorway of the old tobacco factory, second largest building in Spain and now used as part of the university. Spaniards profess to be irritated by the attention given *Carmen* throughout the rest of the world and claim that it damages the image of Spain, but I have noticed that whenever a Spanish impresario needs a full house, he puts on *Carmen*. One of the greatest performances came in the bullring at Sevilla; when the brigands filtered onto the stage they came with lanterns from all parts of the ring, and in the gala scenes carriages with prancing horses and three hundred extras filled the ring. Say the Spanish intellectuals with resignation, '*Carmen* is the cross each Spaniard has to bear.' But others confess, 'We're just bitter that it took two Frenchmen to invent her.'"

The romance and excitement that Prosper Mérimée found in Sevilla in 1830, and which later inspired him to write *Carmen,* are even today there to be savored by the perceptive tourist. What I wrote in *Iberia* almost twenty years ago still holds true: "One of the top experiences a traveler can have in Spain is to visit Sevilla for Holy Week, which ends at Easter, and the *feria* that follows. I suppose there is nothing in the world to surpass this, not Mardi Gras at New Orleans nor the Palio in Siena when the exuberance of the Renaissance is re-created. Carnaval in Rio de Janeiro is an epic of noise and color, and for sheer celebration it would be hard to equal Bastille Day in Tahiti, when the island goes mad for two weeks; but these events lack spiritual depth.

"In Sevilla each spring one finds combined within the span of a few weeks six major diversions: the world's most profound religious spectacle plus a rustic fair recalling those of thousands of years ago, plus a congregation of circuses drawn from all parts of Europe, plus a bizarre open-air carnival, plus a daily program of social events and stunning promenades on horseback, plus a series of first-rate bullfights conducted in Spain's most beautiful plaza. And these six features are encapsulated, as it were, within the confines of an ancient city studded with handsome buildings, narrow streets where only pedestrians are allowed and exquisite vistas along riverbanks. At any time of the year Sevilla is a distinguished city, but during Holy Week and the days that follow it is without peer.

"I have attended several of Sevilla's spring celebrations, and when I try to recall the essence of what I saw I picture myself standing at four o'clock in the morning at the entrance to the tobacco factory where Carmen spun her smoky web to entangle a soldier. I am in a very old city and it is dark, for winter has only just ended and the early rising sun has not yet returned, but along the horizon to the south a dull glow is visible, as if fields were being burned off before the planting.

"No prudent farmer accounts for those fires. In a tree-lined park on the edge of the city, Sevilla is holding revelry and the lights will continue until dawn and for half a dozen dawns to follow, and if one listens closely he can hear, coming to him over the intervening space, the muffled sound of carnival and circus, of promenade and castanets.

"But it is neither this beautiful glow on the horizon that I remember as the characteristic of Sevilla when I am away from the city nor the sound of the revelry. It is the shadowy approach of figures looming out of the dusk as they wander past the tobacco factory on their way home from the festival. They come like ghosts of ancient Spain, from Roman times or Visigothic or Arabic or medieval Christian, moving in stately silence until some member of the group begins to softly clap his hands. And it is then that the sound of Sevilla, the sweet memorable sound of this most dramatic of the Spanish cities, overtakes me.

"The hands I hear do not clap as they would at a football game nor even at a flamenco party. They tap in seductive night rhythm, with variations which a person reared in Massachusetts or Stockholm could not devise. They tap out the beat of some old song, well known to all in the crowd, and before long a woman walking through the night adds her staccato. Others follow, and soon one has along the broad street before Carmen's tobacco factory a dozen or so persons clapping out this strange rhythm.

"No one sings. No one chants the words of the mute song. There is only the soft clapping of some dozen pairs of unseen hands, but I get the impression that the participants are softly repeating words to themselves as they pass me. No one speaks, and when the group has gone the sound of clapping hangs in the night air for a long time as the revelers proceed to some point near the cathedral, or in back of the bullring, or at the beginning of the narrow street called Sierpes (serpents), where they break apart, each member going to his home to sleep for a few hours before the next day begins.

"But before the first group has reached the point of separation, other groups have come along the lovely dark street, which in the growing twilight looks much as it did in the days of Carmen, and they too clap softly in the night. And for more than a week, for almost twenty-four hours each day, the visitor to Sevilla will hear this compelling tattoo. It is the sound of Sevilla in spring, one of the most persuasive sounds I have ever heard."

It was on such a spring evening in Sevilla at the studio of American matador-painter John Fulton that I met Robert Vavra, author of this book and of the photographs in *Iberia,* in which I described my introduction to him: "Gradually as I visited John Fulton more often, I became aware of a quiet young man who seemed to be sharing the apartment and to be decorating it with photographs of high quality. For long periods, when the talk was on subjects in which I had little interest, I would study the photographs, excellent works in very dark blacks and pure whites, and I became convinced that the man who had taken them understood Spain.

"The quiet young fellow with well-fitted suits and conservative haircut was Robert Vavra, from California, a nature photographer. He had been working for some years on a book of text and pictures describing in detail the life and death of the fighting bull, and from the first moment I saw his work in sequence I was convinced that here was a man who could photograph the movement and sense of animals; but I was equally impressed by his shots of people. He seemed to catch the spirit of things in repose; there was little artiness about him and I began to look forward to my visits to the apartment: I wanted to see what Vavra had done recently.

"There followed a chain of unforgettable days in Las Marismas, tracking bulls, watching wildlife and marking the migration of birds to Africa. It was on such trips that I renewed my acquaintance with the bee-eater, that spectacular bird which was to become so important to me when I worked in Israel. Here, too, I saw my first hoopoe bird, which would be even more important.

"Then one day, as I studied a batch of Vavra's photographs and listened to his plans for a series of books in color, a project which has happily come to fulfillment, I happened to see a chance arrangement of some twenty or thirty fine photographs depicting the people and life of Spain: they were not the usual body of material, for there were no cathedrals, no medieval houses and no flamenco dancers. There was simply the look of Spain, static and persuasively alive, and in that moment not far from the Court of the Orange Trees *Iberia* was born.

"Because I was burdened with a heavy schedule that would keep me busy for some years, I could not then speak to Vavra of my incipient plans; but when my work was completed I went back to Sevilla, and in that same quiet and delightful period between Holy Week and carnival, when the gypsies were again preparing to trade horses on the riverbank, I proposed that we do *Iberia* together.

"I remember the commission we agreed upon: 'Vavra will go over Spain guided only by his own eye, completely indifferent as to what Michener may write or think or prefer. Shoot a hundred of the very finest pictures he can find and make them his interpretations of Spain. If he can succeed in this, the pictures will fit properly into any text. But Vavra must avoid trying to guess what someone else wants. Make others see what he has seen.'

"For the capacity to see a foreign country is extremely rare; hardly one person in a thousand can do this, so that all the vast sums of money spent by Pan American and Air France in their enticing advertisements—'See Lebanon. See Egypt. See Brazil'—are largely wasted, because the people who fly forth to see these places rarely do. Vavra can see.

"Even if Sevilla had no Don Juan and no *feria,* it would still throw down a unique challenge. Outwardly it strikes the visitor as a congenial place, but inwardly it permits no stranger to penetrate its secrets. It is not a city of contrasts; it is a city of contradictions, enticing but withdrawn, alluring but arrogant, modern in appearance but eighteenth century in attitude. In Madrid or Barcelona the stranger has some hope of forming friendships which will uncover something of the workings of Spanish life, but in Sevilla this happens so infrequently as to constitute a miracle when it does. The symbol of Sevilla is the *caseta,* brightly illuminated and with its front wall removed so that the passerby can observe the festivity of a closely knit family group. If he is lucky enough to own a horse, he can even rely on a traditional sherry if he stops outside. But to enter the *caseta* and to participate in the mystery that surrounds the family of southern Spain seems almost impossible.

"Sevilla is a feminine city, as compared to masculine Madrid and Barcelona, but if one finds here the ingratiating femininity of grillwork on balconies and grace in small public squares, one finds also the forbidding femininity of a testy old dowager set in her preferences and self-satisfied in her behavior. It is not by accident that Sevilla has always been most loyal to movements that in the rest of Spain are in decline.

"For example, at repeated points in history Sevilla has been faithful to the crown when other cities have not; the symbol of Sevilla is the rubric NO-8-DO, in which what looks to be an 8 is really a skein *(madeja),* so that the whole reads: 'No madejado' (She had not abandoned me), referring to a time when a king in trouble appealed to Sevilla for help. The city also adheres to an older interpretation of religion and to feudalism. In the countryside surrounding Sevilla the relation of noble to peasant is much the same as it was in England in 1400. Laws of course proclaim otherwise, but custom prevails.

"Sevilla is ancient and as a city of importance nearly two thousand years older than Madrid. It was an important Roman center, and near its present site stand the excavated ruins of a considerable city named Itálica. But the Roman occupation of the area left little imprint on Sevilla, although Sevilla made considerable impression on Rome, having contributed two of the principal Caesars, Hadrian and Trajan. Sevilla was also a major capital of the Moors, having been occupied by them in one capacity or another for 536 years, yet today one finds in the city even fewer of the Muslim memories that make Córdoba and Granada such noble testaments to the Moorish influence in Spanish history. Even the graceful Giralda has had its Moorish origin submerged in Christian additions, while in the nave of the massive cathedral the Moorish pillars are lost in heavy Gothic shadows. Whenever a conquerer departed, Sevilla quickly reestablished itself as a Spanish city, jealous of its prerogatives and marvelously insular in its attitudes. If one seeks a whole body of people who have refused to acknowledge the advent of change, few can compare with the citizens of Sevilla.

"Of all the cities involved in the Spanish Civil War, Sevilla was modified least by the experience; the governors required only a few hours to make up their minds as to which side they were on, and after an initial slaughter of six thousand, took over the place for General Franco and his troops. Avoiding the agonizing indecision that paralyzed and even doomed other cities, the people of Sevilla almost avoided the war. Little of moment happened here and the return to

peace was accomplished more quickly than in any other city of comparable size. To Americans, whether from north or south, Sevilla is of special interest because although the colonies of Spain were conquered by Extremadura, they were governed from Sevilla; the cargoes of gold from Peru and Mexico were brought up the Guadalquivir to the docks where the bullring now stands, and the nobles who were to rule the distant lands either well or poorly sailed with their commissions from this port. Scholars have long believed that one day the inexhaustible depositories of Sevilla will produce hitherto unknown documents relating the early history of the Americas, and they expect maps to be uncovered which will alter our present understandings, for to Sevilla came reports from all parts of the world. Here also centered the branches of the Church dealing with America and the administrative cadres, both civil and military, responsible for actual governing. Sevilla might properly be termed the historic capital of the Americas; during some three centuries it was the nerve center which controlled all.

"If a stranger could inspect but one city in Spain and if he wished to acquire therefrom a reasonable comprehension of what the nation as a whole was like, I think he would be well advised to spend his time in Sevilla, for this city, even though it is too individualistic to be called a microcosm of the whole, is nevertheless a good introduction to classical Spanish life. I was familiar with the rest of Spain before I saw Sevilla, but nothing I had learned elsewhere taught me so much about Spanish behavior. Others have reported a similar experience, for Sevilla does not have *ambiente;* it is *ambiente,* and nowhere has this been better expressed than in a lyric by Manuel Machado, written in this century, which is quoted constantly throughout Spain. It is a litany of Andalusian names, each described with its most typical appositives, except one, for which no adjectives or nouns suffice:

> Cádiz, salada claridad,
> Granada, agua oculta que llora.
> Romana y mora, Córdoba callada,
> Málaga, contaora,
> Almería, dorada.
> Plateado Jaén.
> Huelva, la orilla de las tres caravelas.
> Y Sevilla.

(Cádiz, salt-laden brilliance/ Granada, hidden waters that weep./ Roman and Moorish, silent Córdoba/ Málaga, flamenco singer,/ Almería the golden,/ Silvery Jaén./ Huelva, the shore of the three caravels [of Columbus]./ And Sevilla.)"

From this collection of photographs the reader can see that Robert Vavra is one of the few foreigners who has gotten past the iron grillwork and into the Sevilla whose fascinations attracted Mérimée over a hundred and fifty years ago and which inspired Bizet to write the world's most popular opera.

—JAMES A. MICHENER

PART I: The Sevilla of Carmen

THE PASSION OF SEVILLA

Even today, I can barely conceive my good fortune in being swept away by the glorious current that carried me to Spain in 1958. That I would one day live in Sevilla within a three-minute walk of the tobacco factory where José met Carmen. That almost every afternoon I would stroll the Calle Sierpes down which José had led his gypsy prisoner before allowing her to escape from him. That Triana, where Lillas Pastia sold fried fish and where Bizet's lovers rendezvoused, could be seen from the roof of my studio, which sat practically in the shadow of the Giralda tower. That the Maestranza bullring where José killed Carmen was only two minutes by foot from my front door. That I would travel for years with matadors and know smugglers who sneaked their contraband by night from Gibraltar into Spain. That in a gypsy flamenco dive I would see a dancing girl who was named Carmen and who fit perfectly Prosper Mérimée's description of his heroine. That I would fall in love with her and that after our one-year affair she would run off with a former torero. All of these wonderful Spanish experiences in my life would have seemed as improbable to me as a trip to the moon when, at the age of nine, I was first indirectly introduced to the city that for the past twenty-six years has been my home.

My introduction to Sevilla and to *Carmen* took place in California as I sat on a bench under the old pepper tree at Glendale's Columbus Grammar School, while, to Bizet's unmistakable melody, some of my fourth-grade classmates chorused, "Toreadora, don't spit on the floora. Use the cuspidora; that's what it's fora." None of us had ever seen an opera and, if asked, would have been unable to define the word. However, we, like millions of other Americans who couldn't distinguish a contralto from a·soprano, did know Bizet's bullfighter's song. Years later, I would find *Carmen* not only to be my favorite opera and the world's most popular one, but from start to finish near perfect in its construction.

What was the magic of Sevilla? What sort of rich and dramatic city-village was it that not only induced Mérimée to write the novella that inspired Bizet but also served as the setting for half a dozen other major operas? A hundred and twenty years ago London, Paris, Rome—maybe even Madrid—were fairly accessible to the well-heeled traveler. But Sevilla was remote, stuck away in the southern part of a country that to most civilized people seemed more a part of Africa than of a Europe that "ended at the Pyrénées."

So why was Beethoven's *Fidelio* set in Sevilla, and Mozart's *Marriage of Figaro* and *Don Giovanni*, and Rossini's *Barber of Seville*, and Verdi's *Force of Destiny,* and Bizet's *Carmen*? Was it only because author-travelers like Mérimée and Dumas were seduced by the romance of the Mediterranean to create backdrops so enticing and characters so passionate that grand opera seemed their true destiny?

Still, this does not explain why Sevilla, Sevilla, Sevilla, again and again. Why not Arles or Venice or Tangier or even Córdoba? Part of the answer lies in Sevilla's uniqueness and insularity, both of which are so pronounced that even today, more than one hundred and forty years after Mérimée visited this city, it is still *Carmen*'s Sevilla. Recently, when *The New York Times Sunday Magazine* selected fourteen places in all the world that have most appeal to the sophisticated traveler, Sevilla was one of its choices.

Architecturally, Sevilla is a fairyland. When I arrived here in the spring of 1959, I found myself in a place of such dreamlike beauty and one that was so romantically Spanish that I felt I had been dropped onto the old *Blood and Sand* set at 20th Century-Fox, except that here the jasmine smelled of jasmine and the matadors killed their bulls. The Giralda Tower, the Barrio Santa Cruz, the Alcázar, the Tower of Gold, the tobacco factory, and María Luisa Park and dozens of convents, churches, and palaces make Sevilla attractive, but marble and stone, iron grillwork and tile do not account for its distinctive flavor. What makes Sevilla Sevilla is the passion of its inhabitants—the Sevillanos—of whom Carmen is the most renowned.

As James Michener testifies, Sevillanos have always resisted change. In fact, I am aware of no other semicivilized city in the world whose occupants have so opposed outside influence; many of them felt and still feel that their city is the center of the universe. On the radio in this country one hears countless popular songs with the lyrics "*Viva España!* There is no place like Spain. Spain is the most beautiful." True, few peoples in the world are as nationalistic as the Spaniards, but Spanish national pride is surpassed by Spanish regional pride. Not only do Andaluces detest Catalanes, but within Andalucía Sevillanos loathe Cordobeses and within Sevilla people from the neighborhood of the Ciudad Jardín cannot stand those from Triana and the Trianeros have an aversion to anyone across the river.

Despite all this, however, Sevilla has changed. In fact, it would not be an exaggeration to say that in the past fifteen years, from 1970 to 1985, it has changed more than in the one hundred and forty years from 1840, when Mérimée visited here, to 1970. Primitive means of communication, traveler discomforts, politics and censorship sealed Spain off from the outside world until after World War II. Then, the Marshall Plan, along with the U.S.-Spanish military base agreements and—perhaps more than anything—television, opened Spanish eyes to middle-class affluence and a way of life not to be found on the Iberian Peninsula. Even when I arrived here twenty-seven years ago, the only music on the radio was flamenco. Sevillanos dressed solely in somber colors and women in mourning wore black for life. All men, except for common laborers, dressed in ties, vests, and coats even during the 120-degree August months, and until the early 1950s men were not allowed topless on public beaches. Levis were something that Spaniards saw only in Westerns and I was laughed at when I wore them. Women did not smoke or frequent bars. The masculinity of any man who parted his hair on the left was suspect. People of the lower classes were easily distinguished from affluent Sevillanos by their inferior dress. A maid, for example, would never be confused on the street with her señora. Most male Sevillanos spit on the tiles of their homes with the same abandon with which they dropped their cigarette butts and ashes on the floor. No man of any character would consider marrying a nonvirgin. Few middle-class married males would ever allow another man—other than a family member—to sleep under their roof for fear of what the neighbors might say. No woman would ever touch or water a plant during her menstrual period because she was convinced the contact would kill it. No Sevillano would think of bathing, washing his face, or shaving after eating for fear that the contact with water would "cut his digestion" and result in immediate death. These are only a few examples of how I found Sevilla and its inhabitants in 1959 and how Mérimée must have found them in 1830.

Today one hears practically daily, both from Sevillanos and from foreigners who knew the city twenty years ago: *Sevilla ya no es Sevilla.*" "Sevilla is no longer Sevilla." Now most people here dress like New Yorkers, Londoners, or Parisians. On the radio flamenco takes a backseat to rock, and the city is so crowded with traffic that it is often a nightmare of smoke and sound. (When I arrived here there were seven traffic lights in the city; now there are thousands.) Purse snatching, which was once nonexistent, has turned the city into the petty-crime capital of the world. Sevilla now supports a dozen Chinese and Italian restaurants and, if given a choice, most Sevillanos would watch *Dynasty* or *Dallas* on television rather than a bullfight. The list of changes could fill this book.

However, underneath the bleached punk hair, the electric guitars, and the new morality, Sevilla is still *Carmen*'s Sevilla in more ways than some of us stodgy, romantic traditionalists are willing to admit. I know, because until I started writing this book, I had also fooled myself into thinking that Sevilla was no longer Sevilla.

Superficial changes should be given superficial importance. Sevilla is still *Carmen* as much as *Carmen* is Sevilla. Practically every Sunday, in dark hotel rooms from March until October, matadors pull themselves into their tight-fitting "suits of lights" in preparation for killing the bulls that await them in the Maestranza, the most beautiful *plaza de toros* in the world. Late at night in the old Jewish quarter, the Barrio de Santa Cruz, the soft strumming of flamenco guitars is accompanied by the tinkling of fountains and the overpowering fragrance of jasmine. Gypsy campfires still burn—now around the public-housing developments—as girls dance, their shapes weaving with the flames as heels blossom in dust and hands seem to be reaching for the moon. Gypsy fortune-tellers are still to be found on the streets, and not long ago a friend of mine had her watch stolen by one through the same trick that Carmen used in Mérimée's story.

On moonless nights smugglers still sneak their contraband from the sea onto the lonely beaches near Algeciras. Soldiers still stand guard within eyeshot of the old tobacco factory, while across the river dozens of girls named Carmen make cigarettes in its modern replacement. Usually not more than a week goes by without a newspaper report of some gypsy knife fight instigated by a family vendetta or a scorned lover. Fried fish is still the favorite food of most Sevillanos on summer evenings and in Triana one can find a dozen Lillas Pastias peddling squid and a variety of seafood along with *churros* (the so-called "Spanish doughnuts"). Holy Week, the Fair, and the Rocío still provide the foreigner with the wild panorama of sounds and smells and slow-motion sights that were as much a part of *Carmen*'s Sevilla as they are of the city today.

Most of Sevilla's nearly one million inhabitants are still as interested in their neighbors' business and in gossip concerning the latest scandal about the local "character" as their great-grandparents were. Everyone knows who Enrique El Cojo is and who Fernanda de Utrera is, not only because they are well-known flamenco figures but also

because they are as much a part of their city as Vicente, the crazy peanut vendor who darts in and out of traffic like a windup toy, carrying his basket of roasted nuts. Vicente is as much Sevilla as Isabel Pantoja, the recently widowed singer-wife of national hero matador Paquirri, who was killed by a bull last summer and whose death plunged not only Sevilla but all of Spain into mourning. Sevillanos love tragedy as much as gaiety, and over two hundred thousand of them turned out for the matador's funeral, following on foot for hours as the procession crept from the chapel near the new tobacco factory across the river to the bullring, where the casket was removed from the hearse to be carried on the shoulders of other bullfighters for one

1. The Tobacco Factory where José meets Carmen.
2. The Calle Sierpes where Carmen escapes.
3. Lilias Pastia's tavern in Triana.
4. Candilejo Street where José and Carmen rendezvous at Dorotéo's house.
5. The Bullring outside of which José kills Carmen.

last turn around the Maestranza's golden sand. When this death parade finally reached its destination, the cemetery was so jammed with people that many of them, trying to get a better view of the tragic goings-on by climbing onto marble crypts, literally disappeared underground as the graves collapsed under them.

Sevilla still vacillates between extremes of tragedy and gaiety. It is as much the matador's funeral as it is the soft clapping in the night that Michener describes. It is also the naïve young Basque recruit who may be standing guard across from the old tobacco factory at this very moment, rifle in hand, chin pressed to his chest. Only his eyes move as they catch a glimpse of some dark-eyed beauty passing by on her way to work across the river in the building full of women where cigarettes are made.

The drawings that grace these pages were, with some exceptions, done by García Ramos at the turn of the century. It is astonishing, especially in those of Holy Week and the Fair, to see how little Sevilla has changed in the past eighty-five years.

The majority of the photographs in this book were taken between 1965 and 1975. However, there are pictures here—like that of Juan Belmonte—that date back to 1961, and others that were done a week ago. Earlier in this chapter I said that what makes Sevilla Sevilla is not the buildings but the people. For that reason few architectural photographs decorate these pages. Fortunately, that beauty is accessible in Sevilla to even the most casual tourist. More difficult to obtain is entry into the homes of the Sevillanos themselves. With the exception of several invitations to lunch at the ranch of Juan Belmonte, I would guess I was here for three or four years before a Sevillano invited me into his home for an evening meal. At that time, practically all entertaining was done in the street and at restaurants: The family dining room was only for family.

In the first section of photographs, a general selection of Sevillanos makes eye contact with the reader. The faces that stare out from these pages could be the faces of Lillas Pastia, Dorothea, Carmen, García, Dancairo, Remendado, Lucas, Mercedes and Frasquita, or Escamillo and his wealthy friends. The passion and longing that lie behind their eyes were certainly experienced as much by Prosper Mérimée as they are by us. Later chapters show these same people caught up in their religion, in their gaiety, in their corridas, and close to the earth in the surrounding countryside. In the last chapter are the bulls and horses, the soil and the people who till it.

But now to the center of Sevilla itself, to the Giralda Tower whose tiles glimmer in the moonlight like iridescent scales and whose long shadow in the harsh, midday summer sun is trodden on, danced on, spat upon, and enjoyed as a refreshing moment of coolness by the people who populate this book and the Sevilla of *Carmen*.

Captions for pictures
on pages 17 to 43

17

The archway entrance of the old tobacco factory beneath which passed as many as two thousand women every day going and coming to work at the time Mérimée wrote Carmen.

18-19

Six of the four hundred women who work in the new tobacco factory next to the river pose at the entrance of the old tobacco factory where Mérimée's Carmen and several thousand other Sevillanas were once employed.

20

Part of Sevilla's attraction for the foreigner is its feeling of permanence. A visitor can return here after a five-year absence and find the same lottery-ticket vendor on the same corner, the same waiter in the same bar, and the same shoeshine boy in the same café. This gypsy woman, feeding pigeons in the María Luisa Park, has been selling lottery tickets for ten years at the Cádiz Station (one of the city's two train stations). Faces like hers are reminders that gypsy matrons like Carmen's friend Dorothea are still very much a part of this city.

21

In Sevilla gypsy girls, as in Carmen's time, still adorn and scent themselves with jasmine blossoms.

22

For more than half of her forty-six years, this bullfighter's mother has worked as a cleaning woman. Twenty-four years ago when Eloísa and her family, along with hundreds of other Sevilla shanty-town dwellers, were flooded out of their shack by the overflow from a small canal, they were moved into temporary municipal housing. Six years later, she and her husband were granted a small but neat government apartment for which they paid the equivalent of fifteen dollars a month. Besides electricity and running water, their new dwelling has a sitting room, three bedrooms, a bathroom, and a kitchen. Installment-plan buying has enabled them to acquire a refrigerator, butane stove, television set, and plastic-covered furniture. These living conditions contrast drastically with those of stark poverty that this family and other Sevillanos knew just twenty-five years ago. Although Eloísa's children urge her to have the "cloud" removed from her left eye, she is suspicious of doctors. Like Carmen she is also superstitious, believing, among other things, that if a woman bathes during menstruation her blood will rise to her head and she will go insane, and that if during this time she touches a potted plant, the plant will die. On the other hand, Eloísa might be considered modern because she dressed totally in black, mourning her father's death, for only two years instead of for life.

23

Eloísa's husband, Antonio, never knew his father, and he spent most of his youth living under bridges with his mother, three brothers, and sister. Today gypsies like Carmen and her friends and family still use bridges for shelter from harsh weather and the night. When Antonio met Eloísa, he was earning his living by collecting garbage, which he sold to farms for fertilizer. Today he is employed as a municipal garbage collector. A hard worker, devoted to his family, Antonio is a football fan who has little interest in bullfighting.

24

When this photograph was taken, María was seventy-eight years old. Like her gypsy neighbors, she once earned money for food and drink by gathering scrap, which she sold to junk dealers, and later, when her children were old enough, she sent them out to work for her. As superstitious as Carmen, Mercedes, and Frasquita, María was convinced that if a man showered or washed his hair, shaved or even had a cupful of water thrown on him after a meal, he would drop dead, having had his digestion "cut." Like most country people she was also terrified of geckos, believing that if one of these lizards runs up a woman's leg, it clasps itself onto the unfortunate victim's crotch, from which it can be removed only by having two hot bricks pressed against it. Some Sevillanos also believe that baldness will result if a gecko "spits" on a man's head.

25

This matador's grandfather was born in Sanlúcar de Barrameda in 1890, where he worked in the vineyards until he married a Sevillana and came here to live on the Calle Bailen. In his youth he was the typical macho andaluz, scornful of all "feminine" virtues such as unselfishness, kindness, frankness, and honesty. He was uncompromising in his refusal to let anything detract from his image of himself as a man's man, regardless of the suffering it brought on himself and the women around him. The proof of his manliness was his ability to dominate his wife and children completely, to have sexual relations with any woman he wanted, and to hide his true feelings lest anyone somehow take advantage of him. When greeting acquaintances or family on the street, like most Andalusians he did so with much hugging, backslapping, and kissing which, though seldom motivated by true sentiment, appear to the outsider as obvious displays of warmth and affection. When he was happy, he had the typical Andalusian charm and wit that know few equals in the world. As I was loading a camera to take this picture, he remarked, "With all that junk around your neck you look more tied up than a Roman's sandal!"

26

This gypsy boy's mother was not only named Carmen, like Mérimée's heroine, but was also a fortuneteller. Today, most of Sevilla's gypsies live in government housing projects around which they still tether their mules, pile their collected junk, build their campfires, and settle their feuds with knives.

27

El Farruco, the undisputed king of gypsy flamenco dancers, is little known outside Spain because of his inability to exploit his art commercially. In this photograph the almost obscured face to the left is that of his son, Farraquito, the eighteen-year-old dancer in whom all of Farruco's dreams were centered. The boy on the right is Rete, a twenty-two-year-old gypsy guitarist married to Farruco's daughter. As the performing arts were once the ladder to wealth and respectability for American blacks, so has flamenco served Spanish gypsies from Carmen's time to the present.

28

One of Sevilla's most enthusiastic patrons of the arts, the Marqués de Aracena, owned the Palace of the Condes de Sánchez Dalp where matadors like Escamillo came for flamenco parties, entertained by gypsies like Carmen from Triana. In his garden, the Marqués stands next to a statue of the Emperor Trajan that may have come from the ruins of nearby Itálica, the city that dominated the Sevilla area during the six-hundred-year Roman occupation of Spain, and that gave Rome two Spanish emperors: Trajan and Hadrian.

29

The Duquesa de Medinaceli who, until she recently gave some of her titles to her children, was the most betitled woman in Spain, poses in her palace in Sevilla.

30-31

Doña Mercedes Vázquez Elena, attended by four Filipina servants, sits in the patio of her Sevilla house, which is not far from the north end of the Calle Sierpes. It was in a patio like this that Carmen danced while José, recently released from jail, jealously watched from the street. Most Andalusian mansions are built around a central patio, which helps cool the house during the summer months when temperatures often reach and remain over 105 degrees F. Like many patios here, this one is decorated with potted plants. Sevillanos seem to have a special feeling for geraniums, aspidistras, philodendrons, and ferns, and for birds, usually canaries, pigeons, and goldfinches. The tile work around the patio is not only decorative but extremely effective against the humidity that seeps into the city during the wet winter months. The foreign nationality of Doña Mercedes's servants is a reminder that Sevilla, by way of the

Guadalquivir River, has always been a Spanish contact point with the outside world. Up this same river, to be stored in the Tower of Gold, was brought much of the treasure and booty from the conquest of America.

32

Antonio Núñez's talent and personality in the ring prompted the famous Dominguín brothers to manage him. However, though Antonio was a first-class novillero, he seemed to feel he should be treated like a star matador. When he still needed the Dominguíns more than they needed him, he demanded too much money from them for his fights, and he also began dividing his time between bullfighting and women. When Spain and the bulls were still new to me, it seemed that managers were overly protective of novilleros, keeping them away from beautiful girls like Carmen. In the arena, however, where inspiration and concentration are so important, the balance between success and failure could easily be swayed in a negative direction by any outside distraction.

33

Few Sevillanos could resist stopping to look at, trying to pinch, or saying a piropo to this tall, seductive blonde. It could be safely estimated that if this girl were to walk the short length of Sevilla's Calle Sierpes, she could expect to hear dozens of compliments of one sort or another. The most common utterance would be "¡Qué buen ejemplar!" ("What a good specimen!"), which is exactly the same phrase a Sevillano would use to praise a cow or a mare. In a country where until recently a wife couldn't obtain a passport or open a bank account without her husband's permission, women in many cases are still regarded as a form of property or livestock. The Arab occupation of Andalucía lasted for hundreds of years, and some of its attitudes still linger on here.

34

Once employed at the recently closed Sevilla slaughterhouse to look after defective fighting cattle, sixty-four-year-old Manuel Rodríguez in his youth was a handsome novice matador who was born in the Barrio de la Macarena. As a boy he was befriended and helped by the torero Diego Rodas. Later, however, the two became enemies when Macareno began courting Antonia, his maestro's favorite daughter.

In Andalucía only death is considered a greater tragedy than a childless marriage, which is not only a blemish on a man's machismo but also represents a woman's unfulfilled obligation. Perhaps because Antonia did not "bear fruit," she became almost a foster mother to many of the boy bullfighters who, a number of years ago, frequented the slaughterhouse. From the time they were still wearing short pants, dozens of novice bullfighters always found friendship and food at the childless couple's small brick

house behind the matadero corrals. Two of "Antonia's boys," Manolo González and Diego Puerta, later became famous matadors.

35

Antonia poses with a photograph of herself, at age twenty, and with the head of a bull killed by her father, Diego Rodas. (The famous matador Wide Face—Carancha—was Antonia's great-uncle.) Surrounded by smells of the matadero, her small house was covered with morning-glory and jasmine vines. In years past, the lunchtime odor of potaje (bean stew) from Antonia's kitchen drew to her table many poor beginning Escamillos.

36

These young soldiers stand guard near the old tobacco factory.

37

This fruit vendor and her mother express the gracia or charm of Sevilla. At a stand like hers, Carmen loaded José down with her purchases before taking him off to Dorothea's place.

38

Manuel Álvarez, known as El Bala—the Bullet—is here shown looking through a rip in one of his publicity posters. The poster photograph was taken twenty-two years ago when El Bala's madman, daredevil performances filled rings all over Spain. The poster shows him preparing to place banderillas, having just incited the bull's attack. The sticks he holds are less than a quarter regulation size, and his method of placing them, from a chair, is unusual and risky. Shortly before the bull reaches the chair, El Bala will stand up, take a step feinting to his right to change the bull's charge to that direction, place the sticks as the animal's weight and force of attack carry it past, and then sit back down on the chair. Not long after he had been promoted to full matador, El Bala was gored so badly that his left leg had to be amputated above the knee. This once famous Sevillano then managed several unknown novices with the hope that, through them, he could again find fame and wealth in the bullring. Disillusioned and destitute, El Bala was recently found dead in his apartment.

39

Fernanda de Utrera is considered one of Andalucía's finest gypsy singers of pure flamenco, or cante hondo. Sadly enough, though, there is now so little interest in cante hondo that most gypsy artists barely eke out a living from their infrequent performances. Her face could have been among those that accompanied Carmen to entertain at the lieutenant's house where José was standing guard.

40

A boy with his dog on the banks of the Guadalquivir River.

41

Rosarito was born in the Barrio of Ciudad Jardín. When she was fourteen, she left school to take a job in a beauty parlor. Like most Sevillanas, she has had only one man in her life: the working-class girl who dates several boys is still considered here to be a loose woman, or "too modern." If a girl breaks her engagement, she then has a difficult time attracting another "serious" suitor. "After all," as a young Sevillano matador told me, "what decent guy would want for his wife a girl who had been kissed by another man?" Rosarito and her novice matador boyfriend were fiancés for seven years, a period of time considered both normal and respectable in Sevilla. Rosarito's kind of beauty, like Carmen's, is not rare in Andalucía, where even girls who are not as pretty as she are proficient at knowing how to make themselves appealing.

42

In prehistoric times hunters were supposed to have engaged in prehunt rites that bear a striking resemblance to the practice methods of present-day matadors. Like young hunters or gladiators, these four Sevillanos train for their encounters with bulls. While one boy takes a pair of horns and plays the part of the animal, his partner with a cape or muleta will enact the role of the matador. The caste mark of Roman gladiators was a pigtail of braided hair worn at the back of the head.

Spanish bullfighters like Escamillo, until the early part of this century, also grew their own pigtails, which have since been replaced by a small braid of hair fastened to a velour-covered cork disk that is pinned to the back of a torero's head prior to a performance in the ring. These youths, like most Andalusians, have a probable mixture of Iberian, Phoenician, Carthaginian, Roman, Visigothic, Arabic, and Jewish blood.

43

As in the times of Velásquez, dwarfs continue to perform as comic entertainers in Spain. Here four bullfighters who appear with the Bombero Torero's comic troupe are about to make the parade into the Écija plaza de toros, where eight thousand spectators await them. Écija, called the frying pan of Andalucía because of its intense summer heat, was home of Mérimée's young bandit, Remendado.

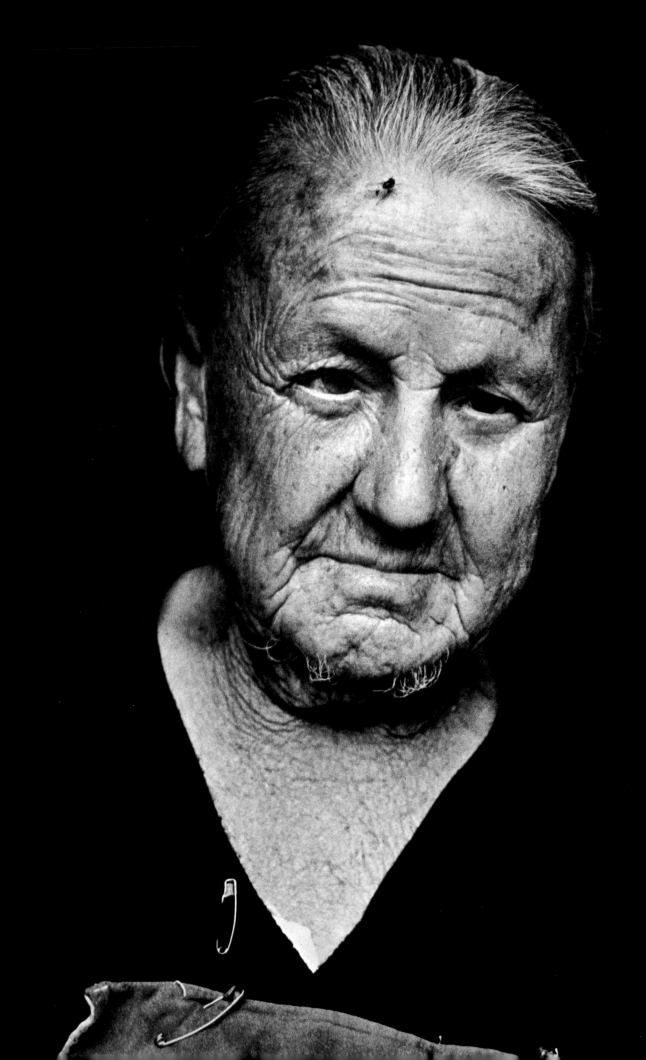

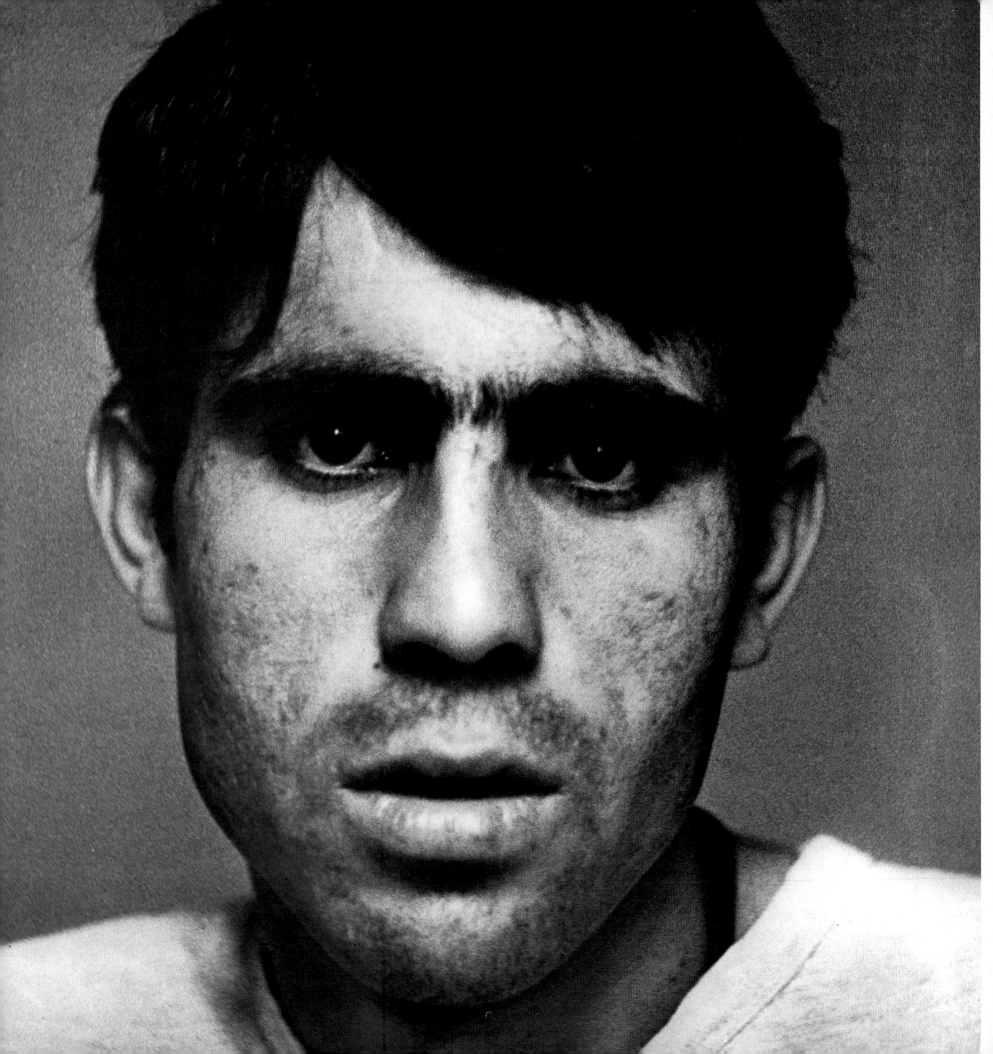

EL BALA ¡¡Unicoenelmundo!!

HOLY WEEK

On any spring evening in Sevilla, especially during Holy Week after the sun has set, the Sevilla of *Carmen* embraces not only its inhabitants but also everyone who ventures into the street, regardless of religion or nationality. For seven days Sevilla is Holy Week, and the visitor cannot escape it.

The oldest life-sized figures on the floats in the Holy Week processions were carved more than a century before Mérimée wrote *Carmen*. Several hundred of them are still carried through the streets on the shoulders of Sevillanos from Palm Sunday until Easter Sunday in what James Michener describes as "the world's most profound religious spectacle."

Each of Sevilla's dozens of neighborhood churches has its own brotherhood, and during Holy Week, the members of these religious fraternities, dressed in tunics and cone-shaped hats, parade before and behind the floats that carry their Christs and Virgins. Each of these processions, accompanied by a band of musicians and a military or civil-guard escort, sets out from its own church and winds through the streets to the cathedral before returning home.

I have been witness to many Holy Weeks in Sevilla, but perhaps those I enjoyed most were shared with James Michener, who is not only the keenest observer I have ever known but also a real Renaissance man.

The feeling Michener had for Holy Week was matched only by his ability to capture its essence. For many of the penitents in the Holy Week processions, Semana Santa is merely a social event when they can dress in the colors of their church and, disguised in costumes and carrying a candle, take part in a parade, slipping out of the procession now and then for a glass of wine or beer. To others, however, it is a true act of devotion and penitence, and no one has described this as well as Michener did when he came face to face with a penitent who had removed his hood for a moment: "For a long, long moment we stood facing each other, and the mark of pain was so visible in his face that I had to acknowledge that here was a man who had truly assumed the burden of Jesus Christ in the moments of the passion. This was neither the play-acting of the men who carried the iron-ringed staves, beating them about as if they were marshals, nor the parade heroics of the armed soldiers looking as if they were about to enter battle, nor the posturings of the politicians as they exhibited their public spirituality. This was the face of an ordinary man who had assumed a burden that was almost more than he could bear; he was undergoing a religious experience that I had not ever come close to, and when I gave him a drink from my bottle he thanked me with an expression of ecstatic gratitude. I have never forgotten his face; he was not of the procession; he was the procession, standing at its very heart, and he was accepting as much of the passion of Jesus as any man could comprehend.

"The whistles blew. The captain shouted at the workmen. The lines re-formed. And the staves thundered against the roadway. 'One, two, three' came the signals, and slowly the Virgin rose into the sunlight, wavered unsteadily for a moment, then resumed her soft undulation as the huge structure moved forward once more. And behind the Virgin, so richly dressed and so wooden with her face staring straight ahead, struggled this weary barefooted man bearing his cross."

One of James Michener's favorite haunts during Holy Week was the Calle Sierpes, the same narrow street down which Don José had led his gypsy prisoner before allowing her to escape. "Because of the manner in which this slim, beautiful street lies stretched out in the sunlight," comments Michener, "it has for many centuries been known simply as Sierpes and has been termed by many 'the liveliest street in Europe.' To justify this, one must accept certain special definitions, for Sierpes cannot compare with a boulevard in Paris or with one of London's wide streets. How little it is! I once measured its width at the Restaurante Calvillo and it was exactly fifteen shoe lengths across. To see Sierpes at its best is to understand the saying: 'The three finest pleasures a man can know are to be young, to be in Sevilla, and to stand in Sierpes at dusk when the girls are passing.' I would add a fourth: 'And to stand in Sierpes during Holy Week when La Macarena is passing.'

"The first evening I ever spent in Sierpes was when the floats of Holy Week were going by and even then I sensed that this must be the high point of the parade, for it was in their passage down this brilliant street that all participants tried to do their best. The rope-sandled men stifling under the boards moved cautiously so as not to scrape the walls. The cries of the captains became whispers. The bands played in better rhythm and the professional soldiers marched with increased precision. At the entrance to Sierpes additional politicians slipped into line, so that they could be observed during their march past the city hall, which stands beyond the exit from Sierpes, and those penitents who were uncovered straightened up so that their faces might be seen. In those moments Sierpes became the focal point of Spain, for although similar processions were now under way in Madrid and other cities, this was the famous one.

"Not many spectators could crowd into Sierpes; on the other hand, since it was the culminating point of the procession, as many as possible jammed in, chairs being sold at a premium. Directed by a group of young Spaniards, I had slipped in and wedged myself against a wall, where the floats passed me by at a distance of inches rather than feet. It was exciting to be so close to the carved figures and to see the nuances of their expressions; there was also a kind of animal pleasure in seeing now and then beneath the protecting curtains the softly moving feet of those who bore the floats and to hear their whispers, as if the spirits of the statues were speaking.

"But as an insight into religious experience it did not compare with my earlier confrontation with the penitent; that had been a true revelation and this spectacle in Sierpes could be no more than a well-conceived parade. However, on Good Friday evening, as I was watching in Sierpes, I heard from a balcony projecting over the street the high, piercing scream of a woman. 'O Dios!' she cried, and all movement along the pathway stopped. 'O Dios!' she repeated, and when the throng was silent she launched into the most strange and impassioned song I had ever heard. She had a deep effect upon the emotions of those who listened, for her voice alternated between throaty cries of pain and soaring evocations of ecstasy. She continued thus for

some four or five minutes, pouring forth a personal song of devotion to Jesus Christ, and her performance was so powerful that all in Sierpes, marchers and witnesses alike, paid her the homage of silence, so that her voice rang out like a bell, floating over the massive crowds. She paused. No one moved. Then she entered the passionate coda of her song, with her voice ascending in spirals and fury until at the end she was possessed. Then silence, as if the crowd wanted to consider her song, then the sounds of the soldiers and the police and the clanking chains and the rustle of the float, as all resumed their march toward the city hall.

"The woman had been chanting a *saeta* (arrow; in plural, ecstatic religious outcries), which would be heard throughout the city on this day. My Spanish friends tried to tell me that such songs were spontaneous outbursts of persons overcome by religious experience, but I found it hard to believe that this woman was an average person overcome by her identification with the passion; she was a professional singer if ever I heard one, and I thought that I was fortunate to have had her as my first *saeta* performer because she introduced the form in such a flawless setting that I have ever since been a devotee. A great *saeta*, well sung, is something one can never forget. But I felt sure she had been planted on the balcony with instructions as to when and how to sing for maximum effect.

"Some hours later, on Good Friday night, when I had wormed my way to a different segment of Sierpes, across from a corner bar which had closed in honor of the procession, I watched as an ordinary man pressed in against the wall shook himself free when one of the great virgins approached. Staring as if transfixed by the statue, this man threw back his head and poured forth a simple, unadorned song in praise of this Mother. It was an extraordinary song, more moving than the first, for it was uttered rather than sung professionally. It was an offering from this man to this intercessor and it was volunteered in humility and deep feeling. Its authenticity impressed the marchers and they stood at solemn attention as the singer's voice grew stronger and his cry more fervent. Then suddenly he stopped and returned as if in embarrassment to his former position against the wall. The wooden staves with their iron rings beat against the pavement of Sierpes and the procession continued."

For Sevillanos, however, Holy Week is many things and to young people it often means an excitement other than religious. Carmen herself may have undergone a sensual experience while face to face with Jesus Christ or the Mother of God. Michener points out: "One would miss the spirit of Holy Week if he saw only the solemnity. In the silent crowd are groups of young girls who would otherwise not be allowed on the streets, and boys follow them. There is much pinching and bumping and hushed giggling, and for many girls their first fumbling introduction to sex comes at this time. As Pepe Gómez told me, 'We don't always crawl out from under the boards to get a drink or listen to a *saeta*. It's fun to look up the girls' dresses as they stand on the balcony.' The excitement is keenest in those moments when some popular Virgin passes, for then the boys and girls press together without supervision and give meaning to the cry that will later be shouted to the Virgin as she returns to her church: 'Oh, dearest Virgin! How I remember you!'"

47

More than 30,000 hooded men taking part in 53 processions in which 104 floats, adorned with life-sized carved wooden figures (several centuries old) are carried by more than 4,000 stevedores in view of over one million spectators, make Holy Week in Sevilla one of the grandest public spectacles in the world.

This Nazareno in his blue hood and tunic is one of seven hundred all-male members of the Baratillo brotherhood, whose procession leaves its chapel near the bullring at 5:45 Wednesday afternoon, enters the cathedral at 9:35, and returns to its church at 1:00 A.M. From Palm Sunday until Easter Sunday, an average of seven processions a day parade through Sevilla.

48-49

From their convent in front of the church of San Andrés, a group of Servants of Mary nuns watches as forty-eight costaleros *(stevedores) carefully move the Santa Marta brotherhood's only float through the church's relatively narrow doorway and into the street. The float's scene depicts a dead Christ being carried to the burial grounds by the saints Joseph of Arimathea and Nicodemus. Other figures on the float are those of the Virgin, Saint John, Saint Martha, Mary Magdalene, and Mary Salome. Santa Marta is the patron saint of hotel and restaurant workers, four hundred of whom, dressed in black tunics with silver belts, form this procession.*

50

This Civil Guard officer is a modern version of the Spanish law-enforcement agents who, during the last century, must have tried to capture smugglers like Dancairo, José, and Carmen. Here he accompanies more than one thousand members of the Siete Palabras brotherhood. Behind him, out of focus, can be seen the Virgen de la Cabeza under her canopy of solid silver.

Technically, only men without cardboard cones in their head coverings are called penitents, and are out during Holy Week for the purpose of doing penance. The other hooded members of the brotherhoods, the Nazarenos, are merely taking part in the procession. In a town of extreme class consciousness, this is the one time during the year when aristocratic and working-class Sevillanos can mix in an equality made possible by masked faces.

51

Each procession generally has two floats, one depicting Christ and the second carrying the Virgin Mary, which are preceded by hired men and boys holding lanterns and incense burners. Some processions, such as those of Jesús del Gran Poder and El Cristo del

Calvario, are paraded in such solemnity that even members of the crowd speak in whispers; others, like the Macarena or the Esperanza of Triana, move along in a noisy, festive spirit as the crowds chant, "¡Viva! ¡Viva! ¡Viva!" Scenes like this in seconds sweep the visitor from the Sevilla of today to that of Mérimée.

52-53

Three of forty-eight costaleros *who are carrying this 9,500-pound float take advantage of a few minutes' break to have a cigarette and to breathe some fresh air. In Madrid and other cities, much of the charm of Holy Week has been eliminated with the motorization of pasos. It is the man-carried float that seems to give life to the Virgin. Today in Sevilla most floats are carried by members of the brotherhoods and not by professional stevedores as was the custom a few years ago.*

54-55

Several hours before dawn this procession moves down a narrow street behind the cathedral. The blurred face (right foreground) is that of a young costalero *who has left his* paso *for a few minutes. The darkened head between him and the penitent is that of a* capataz *who is guiding the float toward its temple. Hearing the* capataz's *shouted directions to the four-dozen straining, sweating men in his charge makes it easy for one to imagine scenes of Egyptian slaves carrying stones to the pyramids or of oarsmen powering Roman galleys.*

56-57

The world's third-largest cathedral serves as a background for Holy Week in Sevilla. The Giralda Tower (past which Don José must have marched Carmen), together with an adjoining patio, is all that remains of a Moorish mosque that once stood on this same spot. The tower with its female-figure weather vane has become the symbol of Sevilla. Almost as impressive as watching a paso *outside the cathedral is seeing the Virgin carried silently through the immense building. Sights like the one in this photograph are what make Holy Week in Sevilla exciting even for the non-Christian.*

58

Rain, which usually falls during Holy Week, had kept the four hundred members of the brotherhood of Los Negritos, founded in 1393, inside the cathedral until minutes before this photograph was taken. Normally, crowds that jam the square in front of the Giralda would have made this photograph impossible. It was a rare moment as the clouds parted and the procession moved into the plaza cleared of people by the rain. The rows of chairs around the fountain, like those that line other sections of the parade route, may be rented nightly.

Used mostly by children and old people, the seats are avoided by young Sevillanos whose nightly diversion (as must have been Carmen's) is to run through town, from procession to procession, seeing the pasos *leave their chapels and watching them at different points along the parade routes. If it should rain steadily, and if the cathedral or their home churches are too far away, floats that are in the street will be invited inside the nearest neighborhood temple.*

59

What does Holy Week mean to this young Sevillano: awe of the Virgin on her gilded, candle-lit float and of what she represents? School holidays? The chance to stay out late at night running with friends from one procession to another? To most Sevillanos today, Semana Santa seems to be joyful rather than solemn; twenty-six years ago when I arrived here on Palm Sunday, the entire week was observed with silent respect. I was warned not to play my radio even at low volume. Now, on Good Friday groups of youths can be seen running, dancing, and clapping behind the cathedral. Times in Spain are changing—rapidly.

60-61

On Holy Thursday and Good Friday, some girls here still wear black lace mantillas held up by tortoise-shell combs. Red carnations, used only on Good Friday, are pinned in the hair at the side of the comb or in front of it. When I arrived here in 1959, as in Carmen's day, only black or dark clothes were worn at the end of Holy Week by Sevillanos who today are generally not concerned with the color of their Easter dress.

62

As Holy Week ends, this man sleeps off the wine he bought with the proceeds from bundles of scrap paper picked up along the city's cluttered streets.

63

The faces that El Greco, Velásquez, and Goya painted are to be found on any street corner in Sevilla.

64-65

This man is singing a spontaneous song, called a saeta, *to an image. The* saeta *(literally meaning "arrow") is a form of flamenco heard only during Holy Week. Some vocalists are professionals singing either for the joy of it or for pay; others are amateurs who if they perform well will be applauded. If a singer does not meet the crowd's approval, however, he may be hissed silent. Saetas are sung either from the street or from balconies and are sure to be heard near the church of San Roman shortly before noon on Good Friday, as the Virgin of the Gypsies approaches her temple.*

66

Moods change and mix in Sevilla's Holy Week crowds. Older persons naturally take a more serious attitude toward the processions and what they represent than do carefree youths who are out for a good time. Semana Santa offers teenage boys and girls an opportunity to be together late at night (normally, young girls must be home well before midnight). The tightly packed crowds also give some youths the chance to touch and rub against the girls who either enjoy the experience or are too embarrassed, as the Virgin passes in front of them, to protest. For middle-aged Sevillanos this week before Easter presents an opportunity to join family or friends for sherry and hors d'oeuvres at bars and sidewalk cafés near the procession routes. Like bird watchers, many Sevillanos take great pride in being able to identify the colors of each of the fifty-three brotherhoods and in relating anecdotes about the different floats.

67

This four-year-old gypsy boy has been with the procession of The Gypsies since 3:00 A.M. Friday. The photograph was taken just before dawn. The most impressive hours of Semana Santa are those between Thursday midnight and Friday noon, when the most popular processions in Sevilla are in the streets: the Gran Poder, the Macarena, the Esperanza of Triana, and the Virgin of the Gypsies. Together, these brotherhoods have 318 stevedores and over 3,000 Nazarenos and penitents. Sevillanos take great pride in dressing their children well not only for Holy Week but during the whole year.

68

The most popular Virgins in Sevilla are the Macarena, from the neighborhood of that name, and the Esperanza of Triana. While most other floats are paraded along in religious seriousness, almost a carnival atmosphere accompanies these two images. Called Cecil B. de Mille's Virgin by some foreign residents of Sevilla, the Macarena has a guard of sixty Roman soldiers, some of whom appear in this photograph. As her image is carried through the streets, there are shouts of "¡Guapa! ¡Guapa! ¡Guapaguapaguapa!" Guapa, meaning "beautiful girl," is the same piropo *that Sevillanos say to women on street corners. Many religious images here are hailed as though they were living people by the crowds who stay up following* pasos *from Thursday*

69

In Spain, because Church and Military have always enjoyed unity, it does not seem strange to see Holy Week processions ushered by bayonet-armed soldiers. Here a young Sevillano watches the float of La Esperanza de la Trinidad, which is accompanied by the Army's Captain General of the province of Sevilla.

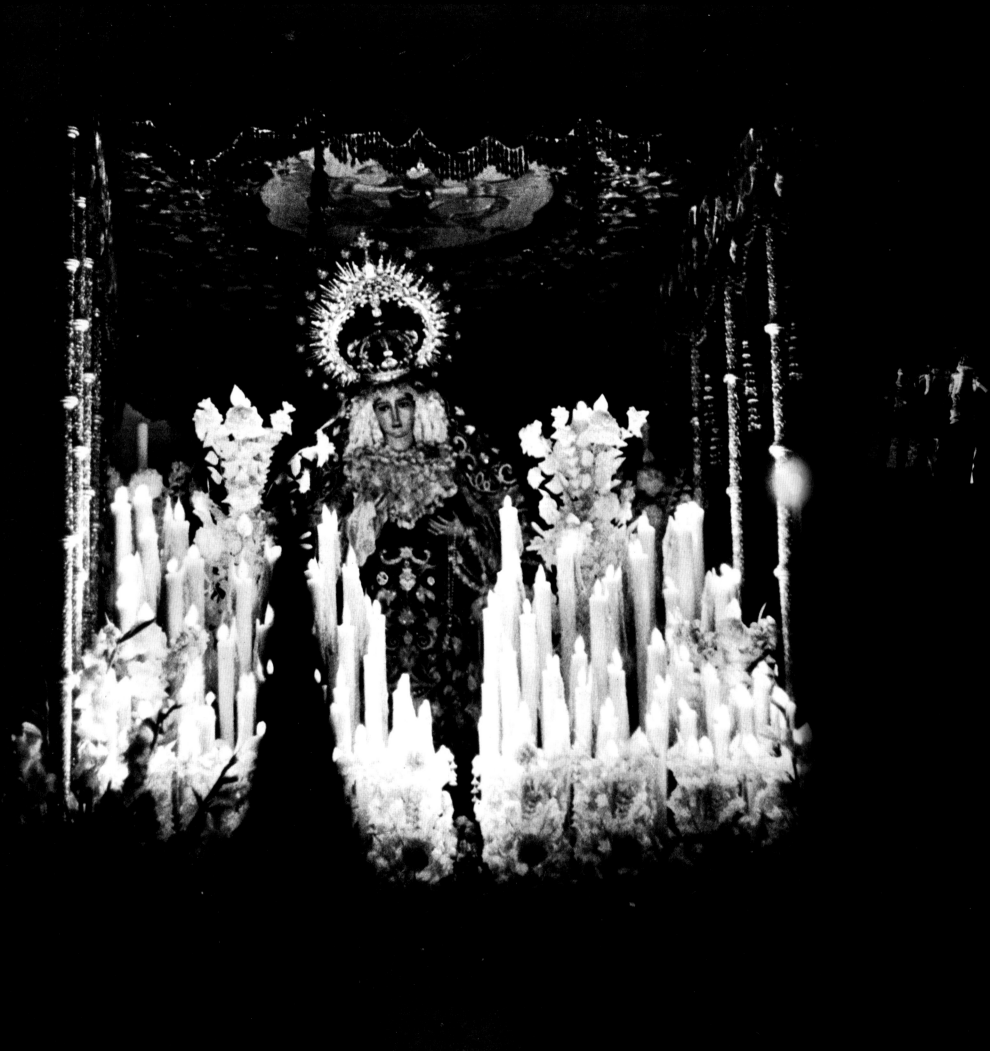

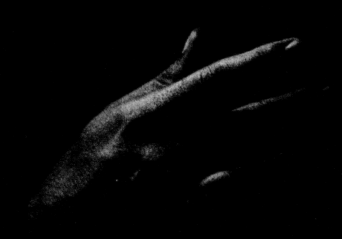

THE FAIR

There is no better time of year to encounter Mérimée's cast of characters in Sevilla than during the Spring Fair. At the fairgrounds across the river, the foreigner looking for Carmen can find her in scores of girls whose dark eyes are set off by spit curls and carnations. Their fingers weave in the air or clack castanets to accompany the rhythms of their feet, stamping beneath the ruffles of flamenco dresses. Here also are handsome men dressed in period costume, some of them in bandit garb that makes them look as though they might answer to "Dancairo," "Remendado" or "José María." Among the military police who patrol the grounds are fair-skinned youths whose complexions and accents reveal their Basque heritage. More than one of these boys would answer to the name of José. One can also find wrinkled Dorothea-like gypsy hags who sell their carnations all through the night—and great is the speed of the tourist who can escape without a red blossom pinned to his lapel. The smell of fried fish and *churros* emanates from dozens of small stands, and though the men whose greasy faces peer from behind the counters are not Lillas Pastia, some of them fit to perfection Mérimée's description of Carmen's friend.

Every afternoon during the fair can be seen one of the most splendid displays of horseflesh in the world as thousands of Sevillanos parade their stallions and mares up and down streets adorned also by teams of carriage horses whose nineteenth-century trappings are right out of Bizet's opera. When darkness falls, groups of gypsies like Carmen and her friends are hired to entertain in the *casetas*—small structures made of tubing covered with brightly colored striped canvas. There are hundreds of them, all jammed together along the streets of the fair. Michener tells us: "It is in these *casetas* that the well-to-do people of Sevilla will spend most of their time during the fair, returning to their homes only in time to catch a few hours' sleep between five and eleven in the morning.

"What happens in the *casetas*? When the front canvas wall has been rolled up so that passersby can see within, specially invited guests stop by for refreshments, drinks and light conversation. Entertainment is provided by amateurs and by troupes of noisy flamenco dancers imported from across the river in Triana. With music and dancing, with sherry wine and *churros*, with laughter and flirtation the long nights drift by. Young couples sometimes wander away from the *casetas* to the carnival area or even to the circus, but by one in the morning most are back where they belong. A special feature of the *caseta* is the presence of children between the ages of four and twelve, beautifully dressed in old costumes and dancing flamenco patterns until two or three in the morning. It is incredible how much music there is in these lines of gaily colored *casetas:* one night at two o'clock I made a casual count and came up with sixty-five orchestras.

"In addition to the small family *caseta,* at which no stranger is welcomed unless specifically invited, so that many Americans spend an entire week at the fair without ever being inside one, most companies doing business in Sevilla operate their own large *casetas,* and some of these are public. By paying a small fee one can sit at a table and listen to professional flamenco and drink beer or champagne.

"Among these large *casetas* stands one with special importance. It belongs to the Aero Club and its membership is so highly restricted that it constitutes, during the season of the fair, the focus of Spanish society. Here congregate those especially handsome people who form the apex of Spanish life: the *duques,* the *condes,* the *grandes* of Spain. And they are a forbidding, impressive lot, perhaps the most conspicuous nobility operating today.

"In the daylight hours the side curtains of the Aero Club are rolled up, so that passersby can observe the great figures taking a light lunch or drinking their Tío Pepe along with a handful of roasted nuts. *Condesas,* accompanied by leading bankers, sit at tables looking out into the street; *duquesas* share their tables with famous bullfighters; at one table it's all pretty women and racing car drivers. At night the curtains are lowered and two different bands alternate from six in the evening till four in the morning. During two fairs I held honorary tickets to the Aero Club, and I would judge the Spanish leaders I met to be among the most carefully groomed people I have ever seen. It is difficult, as one observes their old-fashioned gentility, to believe that they are part of this century.

"To observe this manifestation of Spanish society one does not require a ticket to the Aero Club. Each day at noon an informal parade starts through the wide streets and in it participate most of the leaders of Sevilla society. As twelve o'clock approaches, in all parts of Sevilla horses are saddled up and handsome young men appear dressed in formal riding habit. They wear fine jackets with five buttons on the sleeve, dark riding trousers covered by large hand-tooled leather chaps, white ruffled shirts with lace at the throat and front, and flat, wide-brimmed hats. When they have mounted they adjust a pillion behind them, from whose rear projects a small leather handle which passes under the horse's tail. It is on this pillion that the gentleman's girl companion will ride, perched sideways across the rear of the horse, one hand passing about the man's waist, the other gripping the leather handle. Since the girls are dressed in resplendent gypsy costume, gold and blue and red predominating, the couples form attractive images as they ride forth. When three or four hundred begin to converge in bright sunlight on the *caseta* area, a parade of lovely dimensions is under way. For some three hours they ride back and forth along the tree-lined streets, halting now and then to chat with fellow riders, dismounting occasionally to visit with friends in the *casetas* and displaying to good effect both their fine costumes and their well-trained horses. The girls resemble a convocation of butterflies, they are so colorful.

"At the same time other couples are about to join the parade, and they are much different. The men's suits are more subdued. The horses' garnishings are more expensive, as are the horses themselves. And the women, who this time will ride alone, each on her own animal, are stunning beyond compare. They are the gentry, the social leaders from the Aero Club, and all are dressed in formal black or charcoal gray or very dark brown. The women's suits are whipcord. They ride with the reins lightly held in the fingers of the left hand, their right hand turned in against the waist, and invariably their hair is done with austere plainness. With little or no makeup they ride forth, as handsome a group of women as one can find. In some strange way, in their somber mien, they make the pillion riders, despite their rainbow colors, seem drab.

"But even these beautiful women are overshadowed by a phenomenon of this fair: ornate carriages pulled by two or four beribboned horses, driven by two coachmen in antique costume and bearing four or six girls in colorful dress, accompanied sometimes by gentlemen. These delightful carriages, looking like some procession that had driven into Sevilla from the eighteenth century, ease themselves into the files of horsemen, and around the streets they go, back and forth for three or four hours. . . . I cannot describe how lovely and quiet

and satisfying this parade under the broad trees and along the *casetas* is."

The fair, however, like Sevilla, is also full of contrasts and mystery. Part of Sevilla's fascination comes from the paradoxes that abound within her. Most distinctly I remember a night with Michener years ago when he told me about an incident that had moments before touched him deeply and about which he later wrote: "Thus the great fair of Sevilla continues, day after day. Toward dawn on the last night I stood at the entrance to the Aero Club as members of the nobility departed for the last time, and in the street stood an old man leading a donkey. He was not the kind who would own a *caseta,* nor a horse to ride in the daily procession, nor even a job in one of the carnivals. He was a rural peasant come in with his donkey to see the sights, and as he watched the ending of the fair he sang:

'Yo soy un anima infeliz,
Perdida en este mundo atormentado.
I am a miserable spirit
lost in this tormented world.'

And as he wandered off, singing to himself, the tents of the five circuses were coming down, the parking lot where the carnival trucks waited came back to life and electricians were disconnecting their wires from the multitude of little *casetas*, which would soon vanish."

73

Almost two thousand horsemen dressed in
their most elegant traditional costumes, more
than a hundred carriages and wagons (some
drawn by teams of the country's finest
stallions), and hundreds of thousands of
Sevillanos promenading on streets lined with
over a thousand casetas—all contribute toward
making the Feria de Sevilla one of the world's
most impressive public festivals. Rio gives only
one Carnaval a year, New Orleans one Mardi
Gras, and Pamplona one San Fermin, but
Sevilla, just two weeks after it has produced
Semana Santa, stages Feria.

The decorations on the heads of this team
of stallions are one of many reminders of the
Arab occupation of Andalucía that lasted
almost eight hundred years. The head
trappings of Mérimée's smugglers' mounts
would have been the same as these. While
these horses are being held by a coachman, the
owners of the carriage sip sherry in the large
and exclusive Aero Club caseta that serves as a
background for this photograph.

74-75

The Feria of Sevilla is a rich man's fair. Here
thousands of working-class Sevillanos crowd
the sidewalks, watching as "beautiful people"
parade before them. The cost of riding a horse
during the six fair days (usually not more than
about four hours a day) is high. Assuming that
a man who wanted to ride arrived here without
horse, saddle, formal suit, boots and chaps,
his approximately twenty hours on horseback,
if done in style (with a decent rented animal),
would cost him a minimum of almost two
thousand dollars. For the tourist, the horse
promenade in the Sevilla fair offers the most
spectacular display of colorfully dressed
people on fine horses found anywhere in the
world.

76

Here, at El Hornillo, the horse ranch of the
Conde de Odiel, a coachman poses with two
of the five Andalusian mares that will pull one
of this stable's more than forty antique
carriages in the Feria de Sevilla. Also seen in
the fair are teams of handsome mules with
intricate designs shaved on their rumps.

77

During the fair in Sevilla, some women, as did
Mercedes, Frasquita, and Carmen, still wear
mantillas to the corridas held every afternoon
in the more-than-two-hundred-year-old Real
Maestranza bullring. Hear, Juana de Aizpuru,
owner of a Sevilla art gallery, poses with her
daughter.

78

These girls from working-class families,
painted up and dressed in bright flamenco
outfits, prepare to help Sevilla celebrate its
136th fair. In 1847 the tradition of annual
festivities began in what was then principally a
livestock fair at which animals were bought,
sold, and traded. The dresses these girls wear
are similar to the clothes worn here by Carmen

and country people at the end of the eighteenth
century.

79

Many Spanish matrons dress in flamenco
costumes during the fair. This woman displays
some of the gracia of Sevilla as she says,
"¡Chiquillo, te voy a comer!" ("Sonny, I'm
going to eat you up!")

80-81

Dressed for Feria, the Conde de Odiel and his
wife, Princess Christina of Bavaria, pose in the
entryway of their country house. When women
ride in the Sevilla fair, they do so astride the
horse if they are wearing formal country attire,
but if they use a nineteenth-century jacket-and-
skirt costume such as the one worn by Princess
Christina, they ride sidesaddle.

82-83

Casetas at the Sevilla fair are rented yearly
from the city hall by families, clubs, groups of
friends, and companies. Some are humbly
decorated and furnished with a phonograph
and basic chairs. Others are elaborately
decked out with antique furniture and have
professional entertainment. The faces of the
women on the left-hand page and of the
woman on the far right side of the right-hand
page are unmistakably those of ladies of
means. The woman in the foreground, at the
left of the right-hand page, has a peasant face.
Though it was once possible in Sevilla to
distinguish class by dress, the last twenty years
of prosperity have done away with this social
guide. Now and then upper-class Sevillanos
can still be heard to remark, jokingly but with
some apparent bitterness, that in downtown
Sevilla, where almost everyone dresses well, a
maid can no longer be distinguished from her
señora or mistress.

84-85

American bullfighter and painter John Fulton
was captured by the romance of Sevilla, where
he has lived for almost thirty years, as were
Mérimée and other creative men. Fulton
appears dressed for the fair in an eighteenth-
century costume similar to those worn by
Carmen's smuggler and bandit friends.
Fulton's paintings are on exhibit at his art
gallery in Sevilla's Barrio de Santa Cruz.

86

The Maria Luisa Park offers shade and
seclusion to the young, the old, and the
romantic.

87

Each of the Feria's hundreds of casetas has its
own source of music, ranging from blasting
phonographs to live entertainment, which
plays sevillanas rhythms from noon until
dawn. The sevillanas, which most girls here
dance adequately, have roots that can be
traced back to the eighteenth century. Surely

Carmen danced them at fiestas on her
escapades away from lovesick José.

88

On Saturday and Sunday of Feria (the fair
always begins on a Tuesday) the main streets
of the promenade are so crowded that the
horses can often move only a few feet at a
time. On their smuggling expeditions, Carmen
must have sat in a similar fashion behind José.

89

This handsome young woman controls her
spirited stallion with sharp spurs, a Spanish
bit, and an unseen bar of metal teeth that is
hidden under the bridle's nose strap. As clouds
gather again over Sevilla, she and her
companions from nearby Jérez de la Frontera
prepare to enjoy the only day of good weather
in a fair that was ruined by rain. Spring
weather in Sevilla is unstable enough to make
Feria a risky business for those who have
prepared for it and invested in it. December,
January, February, and March are relatively
cold months here, with cloudy weather and
rain that can last through May. June is usually
mild and clear, while July, August, and the
first part of September are cloudless but too
hot for most visitors. The last part of
September through the middle of November is
considered to be Sevilla's mildest season.

90-91

Some of the most interesting figures at night at
the fair are the gypsy carnation sellers and
their families. Like Carmen, these bold and
clever women are survivors in the true sense of
the word.

92

This ambulant gypsy vendor is trying to sell his
copperware to an irate American tourist.
Gypsies lend local color to the Sevilla fair and
are traditionally a part of it. This boy, whose
ancestors felt that long hair was a sign of
manliness, has grown his hair shoulder length
to conform with modern fashion. Because of
their lack of education and their refusal to
lower traditional barriers, gypsies in
Andalucía, as in the time of Carmen, are
generally discriminated against and treated as
second-class citizens—except for successful
matadors and flamenco entertainers.

93

The fair had ended several days before these
boys from the Barrio de Ciudad Jardín dressed
themselves up in the paper streamers and
lanterns of a deserted caseta. After having
spent six days walking up and down the streets
of the fair without a fine costume to wear, a
horse to ride, or casetas to enter, the boy in the
center seems to be wearing an expression of
arrogance that in the fair is reserved only for
the privileged. This pride and sense of
independence, which were so apparent in
Carmen, are basic to the Spanish character.

EL ROCÍO

My friend James Michener eloquently describes the country festival of El Rocío, which is as much a part of Sevilla as Holy Week and the fair and which offers the tourist a generous and delicious taste of the world of *Carmen*. Once, at dusk, as Michener and I sat in a hide waiting for wild boar to appear at a pond in the marshes near the Virgin's shrine, he related to me a history of El Rocío which he later wrote in *Iberia:* "In the heart of the swampland there was a building which I scarcely expected to find in such a place, a stone church which served as a shrine for a dramatic cult centering upon a wooden statue of the Virgin, known formally as Nuestra Señora del Rocío (Our Lady of the Dew) and popularly as La Blanca Paloma (the White Dove). Around the church has grown up an extraordinary village of some six or eight tree-lined streets with cottages on each side, so that the place looks almost as much English as it does Spanish. The village is unusual in that it is empty for fifty-one weeks each year; it is the fifty-second week that counts.

"To appreciate the significance of El Rocío one must go far back in history to a time prior to 711, when the Visigoths still ruled Spain after having converted it to Christianity. There must have been in those days many churches in Sevilla and other settlements along the edges of Las Marismas (the marshes) and each contained a stone or wooden statue of the Virgin, who even then was popular in Spain. In 711 the Muslims invaded from Africa and within a few months overran the southern areas of the country and threatened the others. The Christians, terrified by this unknown enemy who crushed any army that controlled him, grabbed the statues from their churches and buried them in remote spots to protect them from profanation by the infidel. As it turned out, their apprehensions were unjustified because Islam, even though it sought converts, preferred that conquered people remain Christian, for if they did extra taxes could be levied. Thus churches were not only permitted to continue but were encouraged to do so.

"When the relatively benevolent nature of the new order was discovered, many of the buried statues were dug up and returned to their niches, but others remained where they were and were forgotten. Perhaps the man who had buried a given statue was the one who embraced the new religion when he saw that it was economically profitable to do so; if he had converted, it was unlikely that he would dig up a statue relating to his old faith. At any rate, when four or five centuries of Muslim occupation had passed and Christians began regaining their lost territories, it became fairly common for shepherds, who lived under the open sky year after year with little to occupy them, to uncover by accident in some remote spot one of these long-buried Virgins. Word of his discovery would flash across the countryside and before long would reach the bishop in the capital. Investigations would be launched, but by this time the simple act of uncovering the statue would have been clothed in spiritual garb. 'For three nights running Juan the Shepherd saw a light hovering above a rock.' Or 'While Tomás was tending his sheep he heard a voice speaking to him.' Thus a miracle was born.

"In my travels through Spain, I was to come upon at least eight of these miraculous appearances of the Virgin, but none with more appealing history than the finding of the El Rocío statue in Las Marismas. More than a century had passed since the area had passed from Muslim control to Christian, and one day a hunter from the town of Almonte was looking for game when his dogs assumed a point before a thicket. He verified that there was not game in the brush, but the dogs continued with their point, so he investigated and found hidden in the hollow of a tree a statue of the Virgin. He abandoned his hunt, took the image in his arms and set out for Almonte, but with his burden he became weary and fell asleep, only to awaken and discover that the image had disappeared. He returned to the tree and was overjoyed to find that the statue had returned there and was once more in the hollow, where he left her to report the miracle in Almonte. A group of villagers, doubting his story, walked the long distance to the tree to see for themselves, and when they entered the thicket they found the statue hiding in the tree. Again they tried to carry her to Almonte and again she insisted upon returning to the tree, whereupon the men ran back to the village and informed their priest, who explained that by gesture she meant to tell them that it was there that she wished to be worshipped. Accordingly, they raised a hermitage on the spot, which accounts for the remote location of so famous a shrine. She was at first called, after the place of the apparition, Nuestra Señora de la Rociana, a name that was later altered by the villagers, no one knows exactly when or how, to the simple and poetic Nuestra Señora del Rocío.

"As for the village that has grown up about it, a full-scale settlement with many cottages fully furnished for one week's occupancy a year, the fame of the Virgin of El Rocío became so widespread that each spring an enormous pilgrimage is organized throughout southern Spain, when families in traditional two-wheeled carts decorated with banners and flowers and drawn by oxen similarly decorated take the long trek to El Rocío to pay homage to the stubborn Virgin who knew where she wanted her home to be. In special years as many as eighty thousand pilgrims ride over dusty roads to enjoy as wild a weekend as Spain has to offer."

In the bluish purple of evening, a team of immense snow-white oxen heavily adorned with silver trappings emerges from the dusty darkness. The metal on their heads and the heavy silver cart that they pull are ablaze with the twinkling reflection of hundreds of candles. They look like beasts from a medieval fairy tale. Dozens of women, dressed in bright ankle-length polka-dotted skirts, their long black hair pulled back and wrapped in bandannas, follow the silver cart on foot or on horseback, looking as Carmen must have looked on her smuggling missions. Many carry long candles that flicker in the breeze. A band of some thirty men, all wearing Andalusian country suits with broad-brimmed hats, break out of the blackness and spur their stallions to full gallop before disappearing into the dust and night. Twenty more teams of oxen strain into visibility, each pulling a covered wagon garlanded in paper flowers and full of Sevillanos whose hands, voices, castanets, and guitars chorus to the rhythm of some ancient flamenco melody. The smells of horse sweat, oxen sweat, human sweat mix with the odors of sherry, garlic, burnt oak, and olive oil. Night birds scream in the surrounding marshlands stretching out flat and far under the moon. These were my first impressions of El Rocío as I stood in the darkness, my head swirling with sherry, my senses dazzled by the medieval spectacle that was taking place all around me. I was filled with gratitude for having the good fortune—in a world of jet aircraft and napalm—to be right where I was at that moment.

Since that experience over twenty years ago, El Rocío, like Sevilla, has been veiled by superficial changes. It was a dirt road that first carried me there, and the brotherhoods made their pilgrimage on foot, on horseback, and in ox carts unaccompanied by the Land-Rovers and tractors that now smudge the romantic images of the caravans. At that time the thatched-roofed houses at El Rocío proper numbered not more than a hundred; now there must be ten times that many, most tainted by television antennas and some with manicured emerald lawns and even small swimming pools. But still tradition prevails along with the romance and emotion of this gay and often violent pagan festival.

What was once a dust-swirled fertility rite reigned over by Dionysus still appears to be just that. In spite of the presence of the Virgin, wine in flood proportions still flows cold, blood still runs hot as religious fervor reaches the point of hysteria, and young men still invite young girls (foreigners are prize catches because they are all thought to have "round heels") to join them on their horses for wild rides that often terminate in some quiet and secluded eucalyptus grove. How Don José would have despised El Rocío and how Carmen would have loved it! And although Mérimée doesn't mention the pilgrimage, I can't think of it without imagining the clack of Carmen's castanets, the stomping of her feet in the dust, and the sound of her laughter in one of the eucalyptus groves.

Captions for pictures
on pages 97 to 113

97

The brotherhood of Triana, Carmen's neighborhood, leaves Sevilla on the Thursday before Whitsunday, not returning home until eight days later. On Friday members of this brotherhood pass by Villamanrique de la Condesa where they are joined by Don Pedro del Braganza, pretender to the Brazilian throne, and his wife the Infanta Luisa de Orleans, aunt of Spain's King Juan Carlos. In this photograph their sons, Alfonso and Manuel, stand at the entrance to the family palace at Villamanrique de la Condesa.

98-99

More than fifty brotherhoods, some with as many as five hundred horsemen, journey each year from their cities and pueblos to the shrine of the Virgen del Rocío, which was originally constructed between 1270 and 1284 by Alfonso X. This celebration is centered around the seventh Sunday after Easter (called Whitsunday by Protestants, Pentecost by Catholics). The oxcart in the photograph belongs to the tail end of one brotherhood's procession, while behind it rides a pair of Civil Guards, followed by another brotherhood led by horsemen, and a silver-decorated cart carrying the Simpecado (a richly woven tapestry banner on which an image of the Virgen del Rocío appears).

100

The Camino del Rocío (road to El Rocío) is surely one of the most beautiful pilgrim routes in the world. Here a Sevillano sits in the back of an ox cart, talking to his friend on horseback. The tail of the horse has been braided to prevent it from tangling in thistles. When a brotherhood enters a pueblo along its route, the horsemen carry elaborate flags, silver-headed staffs, and standards. Rockets are set off every few minutes and from the ox carts people sing and clap to sevillanas rocieras.

101

The brotherhoods from the province of Cádiz must first cross the Guadalquivir River by barge from Sanlúcar de Barrameda before starting their pilgrimage on foot, which takes them through the dunes and into the pine groves and marshes of the Coto Doñana wildlife reserve. As the horsemen move slowly through this setting, accompanied by the music of flutes, drums, and girls' voices singing sevillanas, white cattle egrets sometimes swarm above the procession while startled wild boar and deer break from cover to flee through the tall swamp grass. Here a young gypsy boy, near a lagoon in the reserve, stops his stick game to watch a group of horsemen. From Mérimée's description of Carmen, we can imagine that as a child she could have been a twin to this boy.

102-103

On Saturday all the brotherhoods, in addition to thousands of visitors, arrive at El Rocío, and with rockets blasting and drums and flutes playing, each of the forty-four processions passes before the Virgin's shrine in a gesture of respect. For me, one of the most moving moments of El Rocío is Saturday night when candlelight processions are still making their way through the dusty streets. Oxen plod along, some pulling covered wagons, others Simpecado carts lighted by candles. Women in flamenco dresses and men in trajes cortos stand drinking sherry under the pine-thatched entryways of their houses. Youths full of wine, with girls riding behind them, gallop their horses up and down the dark streets. Often I had to ask myself where I was: in a movie house watching some epic film about the Middle Ages, or in twentieth-century Spain. People are continually coming into and going from the village. Some, like these boys mounted on burros, sing as they ride and lift their arms in dance gestures. Others, like this young couple mounted on hot-blooded stallions, ride off toward a nearby eucalyptus grove. On Sunday, buses and cars bring over five hundred thousand visitors to the Virgin's shrine.

104

Early Monday morning, as the Virgin's float is carried into the street by the men of the nearby village of Almonte, the crowds begin to shout, "¡Viva La Blanca Paloma!" ("Long live the White Dove!") Often called La Blanca Paloma, which refers to the Holy Spirit, the Virgin's popular name, El Rocío, is derived from Las Rocinas, the marshes near her shrine. El Rocío literally means "the dew." Once in the street, the Virgin is moved by the rough current of men from the house of one brotherhood to another.

105

Screaming children, religious medals, and sick people are lifted above the crowd and pushed toward the float for the Virgin's blessing. It is said that El Rocío, unlike the Sevilla fair, belongs to the humble country people. With their primitive peasant faces, simple dress and boisterous attitude, they give this religious festivity an authenticity that the Feria lacks. In the rough country atmosphere of El Rocío, the peasants feel at home, whereas in Sevilla they are inhibited by the big city and its society.

It seems unfortunate that many outsiders, screening El Rocío through their own religious backgrounds and customs, find the pilgrimage objectionably pagan. Whether or not one is religious, if El Rocío can be accepted on its own terms (part of which means having more than a few sherries), it can provide an enlightening and enjoyable insight into man's religious history.

106-107

The men of Almonte say that the Virgin belongs to them and that only their shoulders shall feel her weight. What can be read from their expressions: Pain? Ecstasy? Exhaustion? Devotion? Anger? If a stranger tries to get in close enough to carry the Virgin, he will be pushed away. If he persists, he runs the risk of being punched and treated as hostilely as the foreigner at San Fermin who tries to manhandle one of the fighting cows in the ceremony that takes place every morning (after the running of the bulls) in the Pamplona plaza de toros.

108-109

Both of these girls are named Rocío after the Virgin whose celebration they attend.

110

Sevillanas rocieras, *sung almost nonstop during the pilgrimage, are a modified form of the* sevillanas. *Originally sung by only one voice joined by flute and drum, with lyrics composed by country people, these popular songs are now written by professional musicians and performed by groups often accompanied by electric guitars. Most of the verses of* sevillanas rocieras *have a simple charm: "Gallop, horse, I'm not kidding you; behind that hill can be seen El Rocío. Viva La Blanca Paloma!" Here members of a brotherhood drink, sing, and dance in front of their group's house.*

111

On Monday afternoon, when most of the cars and buses are gone, El Rocío is again returned to the people who have come in carts, wagons, on foot, or on horseback. Most of the pilgrims wear Rocío medals hanging on cords around their necks. Along the back streets, the rowdy crowds full of wine sometimes seem, except for dress, like part of a scene from the American Old West.

112

The good looks of costumed young women like this Sevillana make El Rocío appeal not only to the tourist but also to Spanish youths.

113

Late Monday afternoon the village has begun to empty as a once-famous flamenco dancer, full of sherry, staggers out onto the street and, unaware of the camera, pathetically seems to be striking a pose for an invisible audience.

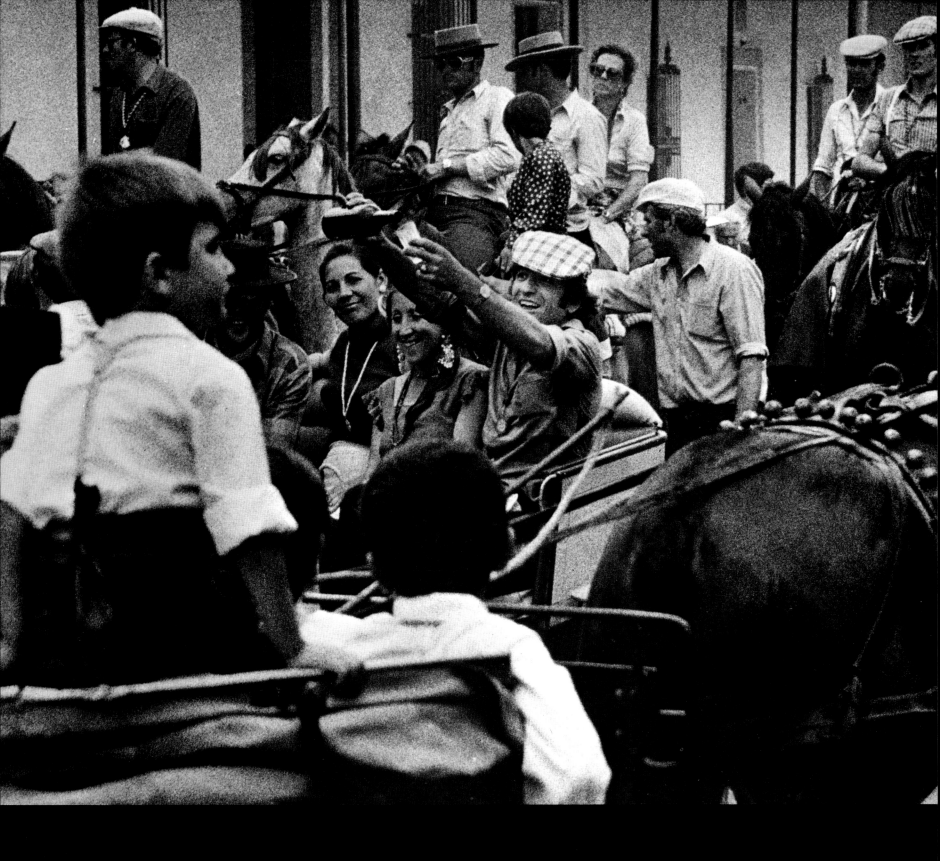

THE BULLS

In France the bullfight is so closely associated with *Carmen* that at the Roman coliseums of Arles and Nîmes, when the opening parade of matadors breaks onto the sand, the band strikes up Bizet's toreador song. The light-hearted French crowd and the theatrical music of the opening ceremony are, however, in stern contrast to the serious spectators and traditional *pasodoble* music of the Sevilla ring where Escamillo fought his bull while outside José and Carmen argued before her death. In fact, Carmen still waits—now in bronze—just across the street from the Maestranza, beyond which is the river and Triana.

When I came to Spain other names in the bullfight galaxy glittered beside Carmen's in my imagination: Hemingway, Ava Gardner, Juan Belmonte, and Dominguín. Fortunately, those were the days when artistic circles here were still so small that before a year had passed they no longer lived only in my mind: I counted them among my acquaintances.

In downtown Sevilla at that time matadors like Belmonte, and El Gallo, with whom I spent hours at sidewalk cafés, still wore broad-brimmed *cordobés* hats and white dress shirts buttoned at the collar without ties. Before I met Hemingway (I had tried every possible way to do so), I told Belmonte of my quest and his response, in light of the importance that meeting Hemingway had to me, was amusing. "Oh, Hemingway. He is a good man but he asks so many questions. When Cayatano Ordóñez and I would see him coming we'd try and hide behind a newspaper or whatever to avoid his relentless quizzes."

At that time, if I had been given the choice between meeting Spain's modern-day Carmen, Ava Gardner, or knowing Hemingway, I would have chosen the latter. In August of 1959 I not only met my white-bearded idol but was "captured" by him—"taken prisoner" as he also termed it. American matador John Fulton and I were in his custody for a dinner that lasted until the early hours of the morning as we sat at a table on the sand at Antonio Martín's café and watched fireworks breaking over the Málaga Bay while talking about kudu antelope and Africa and Juan Belmonte and the bulls of Concha y Sierra—the things that were most important to my life then.

In the weeks that followed I met Hemingway almost daily after the corridas and always found his sensitivity and generosity contrary to most of the things I had read about him. I am sure he was capable of being the super macho but with me he was all the good things I had imagined him to be and more. I still have a copy of the check he gave Fulton and me to help us through a few months rent. "I remember how tough it was when I was traveling around with Sidney [Franklin]," he told us. "I hope this will help tide you guys over for a while." He was equally generous with his advice on my writing.

Those were marvelous days in Spain. Never would I have imagined that it would be my good luck to be in the Málaga bullring in August of that year, a few seats behind the Hemingways, to witness Luis Miguel Dominguín and Antonio Ordóñez in a corrida that is still considered—as a complete afternoon—the bullfight of the century.

During the past twenty years the bullfight has changed—and not for the better. But it is still a marvelous spectacle of color, music, tradition, and drama even for the tourist who fails to appreciate or lacks interest in its deeper meanings and artistry. And if a tourist is to see a corrida, perhaps luck will place him or her in the Maestranza, the La Scala of bullfighting. Few sights are more lovely than this delicately arched *plaza de toros*, with the Giralda Tower rising behind it as the band strikes up and the matadors step onto the golden sand.

Why Mérimée decided on a picador instead of a matador for Carmen's lover is in part a mystery. Although during the last century picadors were certainly more respected and known individually than they are today, even in the middle eighteen hundreds matadors were the star performers. It is therefore no surprise that Bizet and his librettists would convert Lucas from the novel into Escamillo for the opera.

That Carmen found Lucas or Escamillo more desirable than José has multiple explanations. The special appeal that modern matadors have for women must also have been enjoyed by their predecessors, the Roman gladiators, with the female population of Itálica and Mérida. Male public performers—toreros, race-car drivers, jockeys, and aerialists—appear to be more alive because of their association with death. It is perhaps this increased vitality that women find so appealing. I once knew a New York model, a sort of Manhattan Carmen, who came to this country with the obsession of sleeping with every matador in Spain, something she documented in a log of performances and measurements. All women who chase after bullfighters, however, are not as seductive as Carmen, as beautiful as the New York model, or as irresistible as Ava Gardner. Michener informs us that some of them are found to be as unattractive by their Don Josés as by their Escamillos. He relates a story told by John Fulton on a picnic at Roncesvalles. "He kept us chuckling in the mists as he recounted one after another of the misadventures which seem to overtake all bullfighters. 'I was fighting this time in Tijuana and there was this dippy dame from some society or other in southern California who conceived a passion for bullfighters, and this week it was 'our heroic American matador, John Fulton.' As the fight was about to begin she leaned down out of the stands, grabbed at my hand and told her husband, 'I have fallen madly in love with this young man and I warn you that if the bull wounds him I shall leave you sitting here, because my place will be in the ring with the wounded hero.' Her husband looked at her, looked at me, then put his hands to his mouth and bellowed, 'Come on, bull!'"

As sexual attraction exists between women and matador in the corrida, so does cruelty exist between the bull and the men who fight him. What, then, is the attraction for the foreign aficionado like James Michener who has the deepest love for animals and respect for nature? "What have I found in the Spanish bullfight?" he writes. "A flash of beauty, a swift development of the unexpected, a somber recollection of the primitive days when men faced bulls as an act of religious faith. In the bulls I have found a symbol of power and grandeur; in the men I have seen a professionalism which is usually honorable if not always triumphant. I have never seen a corrida which did not teach me something or which did not at some point develop unexpectedly, and I am willing to settle for this limited experience. No matter how disastrous the fight, and some of them can be dreadful, there is the ancient drama of hopeful man and savage beast and the mysterious bond that exists between them."

He later describes an almost perfect fight he saw in Pamplona: "I can compare it only to an opera I once saw in which Gigli, Rethberg and Pinza sang, each at the very top of his career, each in flawless voice. A great deal can happen to spoil an opera and does, but once or twice in a lifetime one sees a *Carmen,* a *Lohengrin* or an *Aïda* in which all things blend in due proportion: the horse performs without going to the toilet on stage, the swan floats get past without getting stuck at the outskirts of Antwerp, the tenor is as good as the soprano and the ballet dancers do not bump into one another, and this kind of performance one never forgets."

Carmen without the bullfight becomes *Carmen Jones:* still an intriguing tragedy, but Husky Miller, the prize fighter, does not bring the necessary element of death into the drama as Escamillo the matador does. Hammerstein's version is highly entertaining theater, but it is not *Carmen.* Without the corrida *Carmen* is not *Carmen* and Sevilla is not Sevilla. García Lorca once asked, "What would happen to the Spanish springtime, to Spanish blood, and even to the Spanish language if the trumpets of the bullring should ever cease to sound?"

Captions for pictures
on pages 117 to 139

117

On the Calle Sierpes a ticket seller stands in front of a box office that bears a poster announcing a corrida in the Sevilla bullring. It is on this narrow street, open only to pedestrians, that many of Sevilla's financial transactions take place. At noon on any weekday, hundreds of men stand here engaged in either business or social conversation. I once heard an Englishwoman remark, "Strolling along Sierpes is like walking through the largest male public lavatory in the world." In this photograph the picture postcard (behind the ticket seller's head) is of the Virgin of the Macarena.

118

La Gitana is as independent a gypsy girl as we imagine Carmen to have been. She is not only one of the few toreras to have killed bulls in the Sevilla ring, but also the only female gypsy to have done so.

119

Once a tall, handsome youth who aspired to be a matador himself, sword handler Emilio González, known as Fantoma (The Phantom), prepares a young matador's equipment before a fight near Sevilla. After trying his luck as a novice torero in Spain, Fantoma in 1924 went to South America where he appeared with some success in the rings of Venezuela. But in bullfighting the odds against breaking into the big time are great—probably one in a thousand—and after several years, destitute and disillusioned, Fantoma returned to Spain. Like many toreros though, he was as addicted to bullfighting as actors are to the theater or trapeze artists to the circus. Consequently, most unsuccessful bullfighters like Fantoma become banderilleros, managers, or sword handlers, projecting their own illusions onto the boys they serve. In bullfighting only one Escamillo emerges from ten thousand aspirants.

120

In bullfighting there are three professional categories of matadors: the aspirant kills two-year-old, second-class animals in fights without picadors; the matador de novillos kills three-year-old bulls in fights with picadors; and the matador de toros, after a formal graduation ceremony called the alternativa, can legally kill only four-year-old bulls in corridas de toros. Matador Curro Camacho is being dressed by his sword handler and by an assistant, in a formal ritual that takes about forty-five minutes.

121

Preceded by mounted constables, three matadors, each followed by his banderilleros and picadors, make the parade into the Real Maestranza ring of Sevilla—the La Scala of bullfighting. According to Bizet's opera, it was at this moment, as Escamillo marched into the Maestranza, that Mercedes and Frasquita warned Carmen that José was lurking in the crowd.

122

Fighting bulls are never tortured or enraged in preparation for the corrida. Their first charges upon entering the ring are prompted by their own bravery, a temperamental factor that through selective mating has been bred into them for hundreds of years. Fighting cattle need only to be separated from the herd to be put on the defensive, which prompts them to attack any threat, regardless of size or shape. Although most bulls are black, some have multiple hide colorings. As a bull breaks away from the tunnel, out of the darkness and into the light of the ring, the rancher, matador, and crowd hope that he will show the result of scrupulous breeding and care by his bravery, power, and endurance. Near Sevilla, this is the ring of Alcalá de Guadaira, a village famous for its bread and, as Mérimée tells us, the source of the loaf containing a file and coin that Carmen sent to José in prison.

123

In the Sevilla ring, this bull is charging at a banderillero who is about to give a series of testing cape passes, allowing the matador a few seconds to study the animal's fighting tactics. Some bulls crowd to one side or the other, a tendency often mistakenly called hooking, and are drawn as if by a magnet to certain parts of the ring, usually toward the door from which they broke onto the sand. These areas of preference, where a bull feels more secure and toward which his homing instinct pulls him, are called querencias. The braver the bull, the less he is attracted to them.

124-125

This is the Real Maestranza ring of Sevilla packed with fourteen thousand people. What must a man like Escamillo feel at this moment as he lifts his hat and, with one foot stationary, does almost a full turn dedicating the death of a bull to a crowd that thunders applause back to him? This sort of ego trip, combined with risk, exercise, bohemian existence, afición, and newly acquired acceptance by superiors, must make bullfighting to once-poor youths one of the most attractive professions in the world.

126

This Villamarta bull still has his strength intact. His head is held high, his neck muscle swollen, and his mouth tightly shut. But regardless of his great strength, the bull never wins the bullfight. Even if he seriously gores one matador, he will be killed by another. The bullfight is not a sport in which two more or less evenly matched opponents are pitted against one another. It is a tragic art in which the bull always dies, except on those rare afternoons when an extremely brave animal is pardoned.

127

Named Carmen like thousands of other Sevillanas, the Marquesa de Valencina sits high above the golden sand of the Sevilla bullring in a box reserved for the families of the socially elite Board of Governers of the Maestranza.

128

Men of the bull world.

129

A bull's shadow meets the shadow of the lance as the picador is doing a fine job. He has thrust out the lance, has met the bull's charge, and is trying to hold it off. At the time of Mérimée's visit to Spain, picadors like his character Lucas were much respected components of the corrida. Now, by the general public, they are little understood and appreciated.

130-131

For a moment there is action everywhere in the Aracena ring near Sevilla. According to Mérimée, at an instant like this José felt revenged by a bull that toppled Carmen's new lover Lucas and his horse. Matadors have told me that seconds like this can be unnerving, seeing the brute force of a ton of fighting bull as it lifts the picador and his mount into the air and dumps them onto the sand, horns banging against the thick metal stirrup and thudding against the horse's heavy pad. In twenty-six years I have watched over three thousand bulls killed in Spain, and I have seen only eight horses killed in plazas de toros, a surprisingly low number when I recall having witnessed four deaths of horses during one afternoon of jump racing in England.

132

El Cordobés is the most famous matador in bullfight history. His unorthodox style of fighting could be musically expressed most fittingly by Bizet's rousing "Toreador's Song."

133

Beautiful women like Carmen and fast cars are the rewards that most bullfighters hope for through success in the ring. It cannot be denied that matadors are irresistible to certain women as are race-car drivers and other men who risk their lives while performing before a public.

134

A girl screams as she watches a matador caught on a bull's horn. Death is present but invisible in other dangerous sports and spectacles such as car racing or trapeze flying, but in bullfighting death is clearly the bull, which makes the watching of a bad tossing or goring particularly terrifying for the spectators. Odds against death in the plaza de toros, however, are high. Since 1947 when Manolete was killed by a bull in the Linares ring, only three full matadors, José Mata, José Falcon and Paquirrí, have been fatally gored in Spanish arenas. Infection from dirty horn wounds is no longer the danger it was before the advent of penicillin.

135

In the ring of Alcalá de Guadaira, this matador, who has misjudged his bull's tendency to crowd to the right, is lifted into the air by the animal's right horn which has ripped into the suit of lights.

136

Having lost sight of the cloth in a high pass, this Miura bull lashes back after the vanished movement.

137

Here a matador, his face smeared with bull blood, rests momentarily after having killed the animal that tossed him. Once some men have raced cars, climbed mountains, or fought bulls, they seem to acquire a need to experience risk, and if they are deprived of it, life becomes meaningless for them.

138

From the Triana neighborhood, Franco Cadena is a young matador who is known for his extreme bravery. One of his favorite pastimes is eating seafood at establishments like that of Lillias Pastia.

139

This woman, wife of a butcher from Cádiz, rarely misses a corrida. She is a grand aficionada, whose faded early photographs show her to have once resembled the young Ava Gardner.

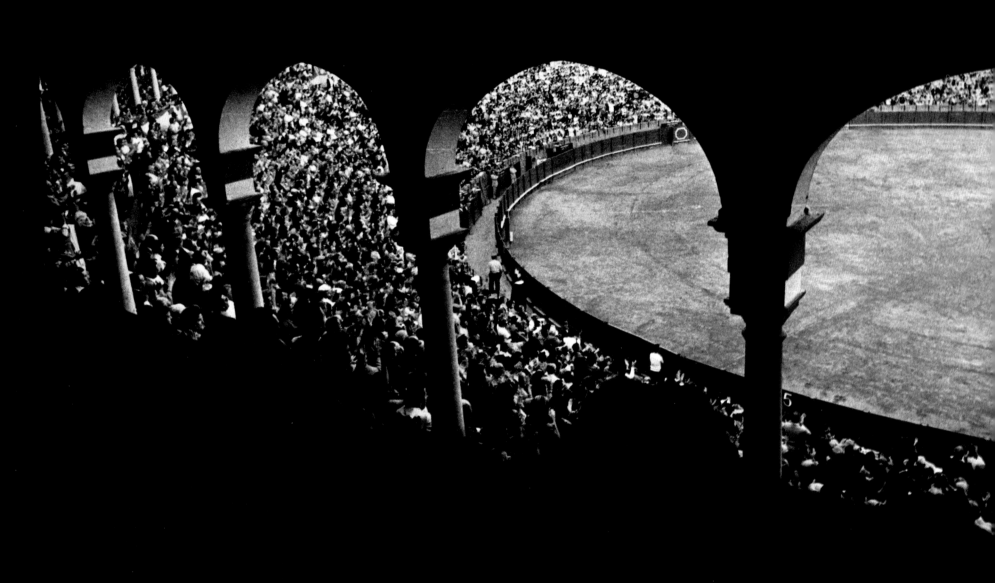

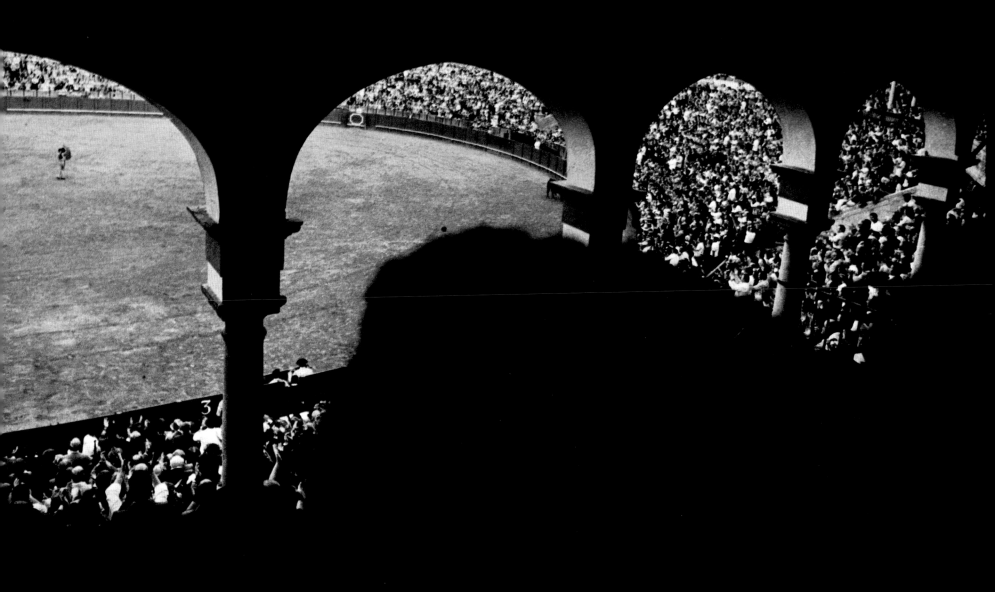

THE COUNTRY

Black bulls. A gypsy caravan winding through sunflowers. Pacing white stallions with shoulder-length manes. Fields red with poppies. Yellow-eyed, ocher-furred dogs with tails curled tightly between their legs. Freshly stripped cork trees bright orange in the late afternoon. A smiling face of crisscrossed wrinkles and missing teeth. The lonely sounds of goat bells at dusk. The sharp cry of kites under the white August sun. Nightingales singing from blackberry bushes. The roaring of fighting cattle in the blackness. The smells of rosemary and lavender. These are some of the sights, sounds, and smells of the countryside around Sevilla that play on our senses as they must have on those of Carmen, José, Dancairo, Mercedes, and Frasquita on their overland smuggling missions in the mountains of Andalucía.

For five or six years I was deeply involved with a nomadic gypsy family who were traveling through Andalucía with their shoeless children and mangy animals. The mother was called Carmen as was one of her three daughters, a bright, sensitive seven-year-old who, if she "hadn't been raised by gypsies," as Don José said, might not have become a beggar, liar, thief, and semiprofessional streetwalker. Those nights spent around the gypsy campfire with Carmen, who was as crafty and devious as her gold teeth were shiny, burn brightly in my memory. Most nights around the fire were filled with laughter, gossip, and storytelling, but there were also moments of tension. I remember fearfully preparing for the attack of a rival gypsy tribe one night. We positioned the mule carts and wagons in a circle around the dampened embers and waited for a dog to bark, for the warning sound of feet on dry grass or the glitter of a knife under the moon. I will never forget the sight of Carmen's husband draped over his bony white mare as it galloped into camp, its shoulder streaked scarlet with blood from the man's eye socket, emptied by another gypsy's knife.

My recollections of the Spanish countryside, however, are mostly of the bulls, those monumental and mystical animals who aroused in me such passion that at the age of twenty-three, with three hundred dollars and a one-way ticket in my pocket, I left Glendale and set out for Spain. As a writer/naturalist I felt compelled to do a behavioral study on Spanish fighting cattle, and as a photographer I was obsessed with capturing their noble forms on film, and so almost four years of my life was spent with the animals I had grown to love. I can still almost taste the cold gazpacho that Asunción, Belmonte's housekeeper, served at the matador's ranch, Gómez Cardeña, after hot afternoons on horseback, open-field testing young bulls before a backdrop of gray-green olive groves. These were the same groves through which we imagine Escamillo riding, searching for the great black beasts he would kill on the same day that Carmen was destined to die. Like Escamillo's, my life was also the bulls, but in a different way, though my infatuation was such that few people I knew at that time could escape without hearing about the stud Piloto or the cow Capitano or the calf Farruco. Now some twenty years later, I realize upon reading some observations that Michener made about my life then, that the Spanish countryside and the bulls that trampled it were of even more importance than I remembered:

"One summer in Spain I had the opportunity to watch Robert Vavra at work. He was staying at the time with a matador and was thus in the center of bullfight matters, which formed almost the sole subject of conversation. Day after day Vavra went into the countryside to haunt the great ranches where bulls are bred.

"For many seasons this young Californian has been permitted by the principal bull breeders of Spain to visit their fields and to do pretty much as he wished. He has stayed with the animals in remote pasturage, and an immense amount of time has been spent close to the feeding bulls waiting for the evocative shot. He has helped breeders; he has worked at the branding; he has assisted at the selection of sets of bulls for specific fights; and he has helped get the bulls into their boxes, not an easy job.

"Vavra has fought the cows whose tested bravery later insures bulls of character; he has ridden to the fights with the bulls; he has stayed with them in the corral; he has helped work them into the dark rooms under the arenas; and he has photographed them as they gave fight in the late afternoon.

"He underwent considerable hardship and some danger, and I recall most vividly the day we spent at the notable Concha y Sierra Ranch with the foreman, old Diego, who loved his wild animals almost as much as Vavra did. I shall not soon forget the sight of Vavra perched precariously on the rump of a horse ridden by Diego as the two passed among half a hundred fighting bulls, each capable of lifting Diego's horse and its passengers high into the air with one chop of its deadly horns.

"More memorable, for me, were the hours he and I spent at the corrals on Saturday afternoons and Sunday mornings studying the structure of the relationships within the group of six bulls that was to be fought in the next fight. We took meticulous notes concerning the prospects of each bull and how he seemed to respond to the phenomena about him. I had done this many times in the past, with others who were reasonably knowledgeable, and I fancied that I knew something about the bulls and their prospects. But it was uncanny how Robert Vavra consistently picked the bulls that would be brave, those that would be cowardly, and those that would have some marked characteristic during the fight. At any rate, I found Vavra far more informed on the capacities of fighting bulls than any amateur, Spanish, Mexican or American, that I had previously known.

"What was more important, he could communicate his knowledge, his enthusiasm and his love. It may seem excessive to use the word *love* in this capacity, but I assure the reader that when one has looked long at the bullfight he becomes increasingly identified with the bull and in time approaches the psychological state that Vavra has been in for four or five years: he comes to love these great, dark beasts, these titanic symbols, for they are among the most fascinating animals on earth, puissant and unique.

"It is this mystical quality of the fighting bull—'the only truly honorable element in this bullfight'—that Robert Vavra has caught in his work. His is a subject that has fascinated men for some thirty centuries: why should one curious breed of animal, the fighting bull of Spain, be the bravest, most dedicated and noblest adversary that man faces in the natural world?"

My days on the ranches near Sevilla would not have been as pleasant had it not been for the simple country people who often fed me and sometimes invited me to sleep in the coolness of their whitewashed, thatched-roofed huts. At that time in Andalucía some of them were as wonderfully naïve as if they had stepped directly into the twentieth century from Mérimée's Spain. Once I remember sitting in the darkness watching the stars and suddenly spotting the satellite *Sputnik,* which I quickly pointed out to my hosts. But they only laughed, shaking their heads in disbelief as they commented that if God had wanted man to fly he would have given him wings.

The person I remember with most affection is José, the foreman at the Juan Tassara ranch. Often we sat in front of his house on hot summer evenings, and while we split cool wedges of melon between us, we would listen to the bulls and cows moving about in the darkness. The owls and nightjars would be calling back and forth through the grove, and then, far off, a bull in the moonlight, black and mysterious against the white of a dry river bed, would start roaring. We would sit, as my imagination tells me that Don José and Dancairo surely sat, eating melon and listening to the night sounds in silence, while the moon rose higher into the sky.

Captions for pictures
on pages 143 to 159

143

A cattle egret tries to keep its balance as a Concha y Sierra bull gets to his feet in the marsh near the Guadalquivir River. Seeking the seclusion of this same river basin, savage bulls, said to have been brought to Andalucía by the Carthaginians, escaped their owners and roamed the marshes in wild herds. The Roman invasion brought Mithraism, a Persian sun-bull religion, to Spain where bulls were then fervently worshipped and sacrificed. Today the bull still holds religious prominence in India, China, Melanesia, Indonesia, Madagascar, and parts of Africa. However, it is in Spain that Sunday after Sunday the sun witnesses the killing of the only modern bull not bred for meat, milk, or work, but for death by the sword in a public spectacle.

144

The good looks of Sevillanos are not limited to the Carmens of Triana. Here a youth from that same neighborhood relaxes in the countryside that is so important to Sevilla.

145

After having tried a two-year-old bull's bravery on the open range, these horsemen attempt to lure the animal from the testing field. Escamillo can be imagined in such a setting on the afternoon before his confrontation with José. This bull is a descendant of fierce cattle probably brought to Spain from Africa by the Carthaginians and by the Romans who not only used bulls in gladiatorial combats in Itálica (just outside Sevilla) and Mérida, but also held them sacred as part of the Mithraic religion. With the Moorish conquest of Andalucía, cattle in the open field were lanced by Arabs. Later, on fiesta days when wild bulls were brought to enclosed village squares to be fought by gentlemen on horseback, the spectators gradually began showing preference for the work of the cape-armed servants whose job it was to distract the horns from their masters' fallen mounts. So it was, at about the time of the American Revolution, that modern bullfighting was born. In Mérimée's day Spanish ranchers worked with almost raw material, wild animals whose blood lines ran directly back to the great aurochs that thousands of years ago roamed Europe and to the fierce bulls of Crete and Africa that were brought to Spain by the Carthaginians. Before the time that bulls were bred on ranches, they were limited in bravery and nobility. Then man dared less by fighting from horseback, first lancing wild cattle on the open range and later in village squares on feast days. When more was learned of bull psychology, animals were engaged on foot, but always with great caution, for their attacks were erratic and treacherous. Later, when ranchers began rounding up and breeding herds of wild cattle for sport, they saw that

more constant and straight-charging animals made for better spectacle and they began to breed selectively for these qualities.

146

The country folk of Andalucía are among the most charming and hospitable people anywhere. More than once, Carmen and her gang must have enjoyed the protection of these simple peasants.

147

Carmen Ordóñez is not only the daughter of one of this century's most famous matadors, Antonio Ordóñez, but the niece of an equally esteemed torero, Luis Miguel Dominguín. Ordóñez and Dominguín are the protagonists of Ernest Hemingway's book The Dangerous Summer. *Carmen became part of a recent Spanish real-life drama when her ex-husband, Paquirrí, father of her two sons, was killed by a bull last summer, plunging Spain into a mourning that can only be compared to the feeling that swept America after the John Kennedy assassination.*

148-149

At twilight these bulls of Juan Guardiola graze and thrust their horns into the ground, throwing clods of damp earth into the air while their hooves flush up insects, which are being fed on by several swifts. The lagoon behind the herd will be completely dry in late summer. Except for the lion and the stallion, few animals are so beautifully masculine as the Spanish fighting bull. Today, although in a number of countries cattle are still held sacred, it is only in Spain, France, and Spanish America that the bull continues to be fought and killed by the sword in a public spectacle.

150

This teenage gypsy girl perfectly fits Mérimée's description of a Carmen who has been parodied by Hollywood.

151

It takes little imagination to place the face of this man among the band of smugglers who rode with Dancairo and José on their missions between Sevilla and Algeciras.

152-153

This is an Andalusian stallion, a breed of horse known for its spectacular appearance and gentle temperament. It was created by a group of monks at the Carthusian monastery of Jérez de la Frontera, the same town where Lillias Pastia sent José to join a gang of smugglers. Born with dark hide colorings, most Andalusian horses turn gray with maturity and after the age of twelve become pure white. Unlike many stallions,

Andalusians, though high-spirited, are relatively steady horses.

154

At the ranch of Juan Guardiola, a four-year-old bull is silhouetted by the setting sun. Since the beginning of time bulls have charged through history having had profound meaning for such gods and mortals of Gilgamesh, Shiva, Krishna, Amen-Ra, Rameses II, Minos, Daedalus, Theseus, Zeus, Europa, Dionysus, Jason, Hercules, Moses, Hannibal, Julius Caesar, Mithra, El Cid, Pope Alexander VI, San Fermín, Cervantes, Goya, Mérimée, García Lorca, Hemingway, and Picasso.

155

Eduardo Miura is the most well-known breeder of fighting bulls in the world. His bull Islero killed Manolete in 1947.

156

This is the last known portrait of Juan Belmonte, the matador who revolutionized bullfighting in the early part of this century by standing completely still while, with his cloth lure, leading the bull past his body. Like Escamillo, Belmonte was a proud, brave man among whose rewards were fame, wealth, and a neverending female following. I took this photograph several days before Belmonte put a gun to his head to end his life as his friend Hemingway had done.

157

This young matador cooling off on a ranch near Sevilla reminds one of Belmonte's stories of swimming the Guadalquivir River at night and, naked, illegally fighting bulls and cows for practice under the full moon.

158

This greyhound bitch belonged to a gypsy family which was camping under a Roman bridge.

159

Somewhere in the Basque country, far from Andalucía, we imagine a woman like this praying for her troubled soldier son.

PART II: *The* Carmen *of Sevilla*

The intensity of Sevilla is such that few artists who visit here leave without trying to capture some of its *duende*. What is *duende*? Manuel Torres, the flamenco singer, once remarked, "All that has dark sounds has *duende*." Federico García Lorca wrote that "these 'dark sounds' are the mystery, the roots thrusting into the fertile loam known to all of us, ignored by all of us, but from which we get what is real in art." Goethe defined *duende* when he attributed to Paganini "a mysterious power that everyone feels but that no philosopher has explained." Some of us who have known the *duende* of Sevilla are like Don José, who, once caught in the current, cannot turn back.

It is therefore not surprising that this mystery of Sevilla touched Prosper Mérimée, the author of *Carmen,* as it has touched the sensibilities of other artists. On the subject of Mérimée, we know that besides being a novelist and impassioned traveler, he was an antiquarian, linguist, critic, dilettante, courtier, and diplomat who was born on September 28, 1803, in Paris. A reportedly dandified youth strongly partial to England and things English, he was a brilliant student whose first literary works, five plays, were published in 1823, after which he became one of the darlings of Parisian society. Eighteen twenty-five was a key year in Mérimée's life, for it was then that he was befriended by Marie Henri Beyle, better known by his nom de plume, Stendhal. The two soon became intimate friends and Mérimée enjoyed a tutelage that would not end until Stendhal died in 1842. Hippolyte Taine tells us that it was through Stendhal that Mérimée became a skeptic who harbored a distrust not only of himself but of society in general "through fear of being duped in life, love, and in science and in art."

As a critic, especially in his historical works, Mérimée sought an objectivity as cold and clear as ice, which he was able to attain to such a degree that even before his thirtieth birthday, Goethe compared the elements in his writings to "those perfect watches, in transparent crystal, in which can be seen at the same time the exact hour and all the play of the interior mechanism."

A strange mixture of contradictions formed what seems to be Mérimée's true personality, which he attempted to mask with displays of selfishness, suspiciousness, cynicism, and frigidity. Facts testify that behind this unattractive disguise was another man, one who attempted to find a publisher for Victor Jacquemont's writings in order to provide money for the naturalist's impoverished nephew; a man who went to great effort to sell Stendhal's unpublished manuscripts in order to help his dead friend's penniless sister; a man who as a senator donated a large part of his salary to an acquaintance whose politics had bankrupted him. Mérimée professed to despise nationalism and patriotism and tried to give the impression that he was a cosmopolitan citizen of the world. However, in 1870, when France was defeated at Wissembourg in the Franco-Prussian War, he was beside himself.

That the romantic man who was seduced by the passion of Sevilla and who created *Carmen* could be the same person described by Stendhal makes him all the more a conundrum. "Prosper Mérimée was a young man in a gray frock-coat, very ugly, and with a turned-up nose. This young man had something insolent and extremely unpleasant about him. His eyes, small and without expression, had always the same look, and this was ill-natured. Such was my first impression of the best of my present friends. I am not completely sure of his heart, but I am sure of his talents. A letter came from the Count of Gazel [a pseudonym used by Mérimée]—now so well known—to me last week and made me happy for two days. His mother has a great deal of French wit and a superior intelligence. It seems to me that she, like her son, might give way to emotion once a year."

Although Mérimée remained a bachelor for life and remarked openly that "women are fickle and wicked creatures belonging to the same genus as the cat and the tiger," he did, strangely enough, have numerous female friends in whom he confided his most intimate thoughts. Among them were Jenny Dacquim (the "Unknown Lady" of his posthumously published collection of letters of that name) and the Countess of Montijo, as well as her daughter Eugénie who became the wife of Emperor Napoleon II. In this country it was said that Mérimée left Spain with a booty never matched by any foreigner, taking with him not only the savage and irresistible Carmen, but also a friendship with Eugénie that would make him a court favorite when she became empress and ruled France for twenty years. The most famous of his women friends, however, was George Sand (Musset's and Chopin's femme fatale) with whom he started a romance that never blossomed. Somehow any positive experiences from these relationships never reached Mérimée's stories, whose heroines are as perverse as they are frivolous, as fickle as they are evil, and as criminal as they are cruel.

As a traveler, Mérimée crossed and recrossed Europe in order to capture the local color that to him was an obsession: "In the year of our Lord 1827 I was a *romantic.* We used to say to the classics, 'Your Greeks are not at all Greeks, your Romans are not at all Romans; you do not know how to give your compositions local color.' We understand by local color what in the seventeenth century was/is called *moeurs:* but we were very proud of our word, and we thought we had imagined the word and the thing. In the matter of poems, we admired only the foreign and the most ancient; the ballads of the Scottish frontier, the romances of the Cid, these appeared to us to be incomparable masterpieces, always because of local color." After reading this, it does not seem strange that Sevilla, which pulses with local color, should seduce Mérimée and serve as the setting for his most famous work.

Books tell us that Mérimée visited Sevilla along with Granada and Córdoba in November of 1830, but where he found Carmen seems a matter of speculation. One opinion is that he relied heavily on George Borrow's writings and gypsy experiences. Another hypothesis is that after Mérimée had met the Countess of Montijo in Madrid, she told him the supposedly true story of a gypsy girl who had been murdered by her soldier lover. This latter theory would support the premise that only when reality has more power than fiction does it stimulate creativity. In any case it is immaterial whether Mérimée embellished the facts of the countess's story of love and murder, or whether he improved upon a tale he heard in Sevilla, using material from George

Borrow for local color. The only important thing is that in retelling the story he created one of the most popular heroines in literature.

Carmen is a tribute to Mérimées gift as a storyteller. As Arthur Symons tells us: "In this story all the qualities of Mérimée come into agreement; the student of human passions, the traveler, the observer, the learned man meet in harmony; and in addition, there is the *aficionado,* the *amateur,* in love with Spain and Spaniards." At first it seemed strange to me—although perhaps it should not have, given the shadow of Bizet's opera—that although all of my acquaintants had seen the opera either on the stage or the screen, none had read the novel.

In the opening chapter, the narrator, a Frenchman, begins a first-person account of his journeys in Andalucía to search for the exact location of "the battlefield of Munda in the Bastuli-Poeni country near modern Monda, which is roughly five miles north of Marbella." At the end of his first paragraph, he adds, "While waiting for my dissertation to finally solve this geographical riddle which is keeping the whole of Europe in suspense, I want to tell you a short story."

As the story begins, he is traveling near Córdoba and meets a stranger whom his guide recognizes as José María, a famous bandit. Later that night when the guide, with the hope of collecting a reward, rides secretly off to alert some soldiers of the bandit's presence, the narrator wakes the man he has come to know as Don José, and warns him of the approaching danger. Before galloping away, Don José thanks the Frenchman: "Farewell, señor. For this favor you've done me, may God reward you."

In the next chapter, the narrator is in Córdoba where he tells us, "One evening at the time when all things seem to blend with dusk, I was quietly smoking, leaning against the wall above the river, when a woman came up the stairway and sat down next to me." The girl and he strike up a conversation and she asks him, "Have you ever heard of Carmencita, little Carmen? That's who I am." The Frenchman and the gypsy then go to an ice-cream shop. "The week before," he tells us, "I shared my meal with a bandit. Today I'm going to eat ice cream with a handmaiden of the devil. When one travels, one must see everything."

Once at their candlelit table, he describes the face across from him: "I don't think Carmen was a pure gypsy. At least she was prettier than any of her kind I had previously met. . . . Her skin, apart from being perfectly smooth, was nearly copper in color. Her lips were slightly thick but well formed, and revealed teeth that were whiter than skinned almonds. Her hair, perhaps, could have been finer, but was shiny black with the iridescent blue of a raven's wing. In order not to bore you with too lengthy a description, I shall simply say that for each defect, she possessed a quality which stood out more strongly by contrast. Her eyes, especially, had an expression both voluptuous and fierce, such as I have never found in any human being. 'A gypsy's eye is a wolf's eye' is a Spanish saying which denotes astute observation."

After they finish their ice cream, the narrator, who admits to an interest in the occult and in Carmen's fortune-telling abilities, says, "I felt it would seem ridiculous to have my fortune told in the café, so I asked the pretty sorceress to allow me to accompany her to her home." Once at their destination and just when Carmen has ordered the Frenchman to cross his left hand with a coin to begin her ceremony of magic, Don José bursts into the room. A violent argument ensues before José takes the narrator into the street and points him toward the bridge and his inn. Once back in his room, upon undressing, the Frenchman discovers that his watch has been stolen.

Some months later, again in Córdoba, he sees the familiar face of a Dominican priest who exclaims, "So you haven't been murdered! Everyone knows, of course, that you've been robbed." Upon which the priest tells him the stolen watch has been recovered and its thief is now in jail waiting to be garrotted for having committed several murders. It is then that the Frenchman learns the convicted man is the Basque bandit—José María or Don José—and he goes to the jail to visit him.

Once there, the Frenchman asks if influence or money might mitigate the death sentence. Don José thinks for a moment, then makes only two requests: first, that a mass be said for his soul, and second, "Well, if you visit Pamplona, you'll find much that will be attractive to you. It's a lovely city. I'll give you this medal (he fingered a small silver medal that he was wearing around his neck), you'll wrap it up in some paper (he stopped for a moment, seemingly to contain his tears), and you'll kindly take it or have it sent to an address where a good woman lives. You may tell her I'm dead, without saying how or why I died."

"I promised to honor his request," the narrator informs us, "and I saw him the next day before he was executed. From his lips I learned the tragic story that you are about to read." And so we move into Chapter Three, in which Don José confides . . .

CARMEN
By Prosper Mérimée

Don José Lizzarrabengoa is my name. I was born in the Batzan Valley in the village of Elizando. And, señor, since you're no stranger to Spain you can tell from my name that I'm not only a Basque, but from an old Christian family. The title "Don" I use deservedly—something that would be confirmed if we were in Elizando and I showed you the parchment that contains my genealogy. Because my family felt that I should devote my life to the church, they forced me to study to be a priest, that I found not only boring but also difficult. The truth is I spent most of my time playing handball; in fact, I loved that game so much that it indirectly wrecked my life. You see, when we Basques play handball, we do so very passionately. My misfortune came about one day after I had beaten a boy from Álava and he challenged me to fight. Instead of our fists, we unfortunately used our metal-tipped wooden staves. I won, and without going into more detail I will tell you that the outcome of our fight was such that I was forced to flee from my beloved Basque country. A short while later I became friendly with some soldiers and enlisted in the Almanza cavalry regiment.

Because we Basques from Navarra have a feeling for the military and learn soldiering quickly, I was soon graduated to corporal. Not much later I had just been promised a promotion to sergeant when I suffered my second stroke of bad luck—to be assigned to guard duty at the Sevilla tobacco factory. Anyone who has been to Sevilla cannot have missed seeing that huge building near the banks of the Guadalquivir. If I shut my eyes, right now I can envision the main gate to the factory and our guardhouse nearby. Most Spanish soldiers on duty there either play cards or sleep. But being a true Basque, I always tried to keep busy.

One morning I was making a wire chain to hold my priming needle when suddenly some of the other soldiers called out, "There's the bell calling the girls back to work." Señor, you're undoubtedly aware that at least four to five hundred women are employed rolling cigars in the tobacco factory. And in the summer when it gets so hot, some of them, especially the younger ones, try to cool off by removing some of their clothing. For that reason no man is allowed to enter that room without a permit from the magistrate. At midday, as the girls return to work, lots of young men hang around the factory to try to flirt with them. The girls who dress provocatively are easy catches for any fellow who tosses out a line to them.

But to return to my story. While the other soldiers stared at the girls returning to the factory, I didn't get up from my bench near the gate. I was young and couldn't stop dreaming of and feeling homesick for the Basque country—and our girls with their blue skirts and shoulder-length braids. Anyhow, Andalusian girls, always teasing with their silly talk, were so foreign to me that I was apprehensive of them.

I was sitting there, minding my own business, working on my chain, when I heard some passing Sevillanos exclaim: "Look, there's the gypsy girl!" It was then that I glanced up and saw her for the first time. It was Friday; I'll never be able to erase that instant from my mind. There came Carmen, the girl at whose shack you and I met again months ago.

Her skirt was so short that it failed to cover up the holes that blemished her silk stockings. The shoes she wore were of the same hue as her skirt and tied with flame-colored ribbons. To show off her shoulders she draped her mantilla seductively low, and she had stuck acacia blossoms in her blouse between her breasts. She also had one of those sweet-smelling blossoms flowering out from the edge of her lips and, as she walked, she moved her hips in such a way that you would have thought she was some flirting filly from the military stud farm at Córdoba. My God, if a Basque woman had dressed so provocatively every person in my village would have made the sign of the cross as she passed. However, as Carmen strutted along, hardly a Sevillano in the plaza could resist uttering some compliment about her appearance. Like the true gypsy she was, she brazenly kept her hand on her hip as she flashed torrid glances at every man who spoke to her. At that moment I wasn't in the least attracted to her, and my eyes returned to the chain in my hands. Women, as you must know, señor, are similar to cats in that they won't come when called but will purr and rub against your legs if you pay no attention to them. So it was with Carmen. She had barely passed when she stopped, turned around, and spoke to me.

"Amigo," she said in typical Andaluz fashion, "why don't you give me that chain and I'll fasten my strongbox to it?"

"I need it to hold my priming needle," I replied.

"Your priming needle!" She burst out laughing. "Aye, if the gentleman needs a needle, he must be making lace!"

I felt my face turn red as I tried to come up with an answer and defend myself while everyone around doubled up with laughter.

"Come now, my love," she continued, "stitch me seven yards of lace for a mantilla and you'll be the needleman of my heart!"

And if that weren't enough, she plucked the acacia flower from her mouth and flicked it at me with such force and accuracy that it struck me right between the eyes. Señor, I was in such a state of embarrassment and shock that I felt I had been struck by a bullet. . . . I remained frozen to the spot. Then I made my first big mistake. She must have cast a spell on me, for I picked up the flower as nonchalantly as possible so that the other soldiers wouldn't notice, and then carefully placed it in the inside pocket of my jacket as though it were the most precious thing I had ever owned.

A few hours later I was still bewilderedly trying to analyze my experience with the gypsy girl when a porter, breathless and appearing terribly upset, burst into the guardhouse. A woman had been murdered in the big room at the tobacco factory, he gasped, and some of us should go there immediately. Our sergeant ordered me to take two men and investigate the report. We got to the factory as fast as we could and entered the big room. Just imagine, señor, suddenly I found myself in the midst of more than three hundred screaming, howling, gesticulating women dressed in little more than their slips. Above this uproar that would have deafened even God's thunder, some of them were screeching at a girl stretched out on the floor and covered with blood, but still alive. Two fresh knife slashes formed an X on her face. A group of the kinder women were trying to help her while behind them I saw Carmen being restrained by five or six of her fellow workers.

"Get a priest! I need to confess! I'm dying!" howled the wounded woman while Carmen struggled silently, clenching her teeth and rolling her eyes like a chameleon.

"What's happened here?" I asked. With all of these excited women screeching at me simultaneously, it was practically impossible to determine what had actually taken place. However, it appeared that the bleeding woman had been bragging that she had enough money in her pocket to go to the Triana marketplace and buy a burro. The trouble started when Carmen with her sharp tongue said, "Oh, shut up, you old witch. When you've got a broom to carry you around, what do you need with a burro?"

Offended by Carmen's sarcasm, the other woman put her own

pointed tongue to work and replied that, not having the honor to be a gypsy woman or one of Satan's godchildren, she was not familiar with brooms. And then to get a last lick in, she added that Señorita Carmencita would soon make the acquaintance of her burro when the police placed her on the animal and drove her out of town as is done with all prostitutes, with two stooges running behind to shoo the flies from her.

Then Carmen said, "Those flies may be thirsty, so I'd better make some drinking troughs for them on her cheek. I'm going to draw a checkerboard on it right now." And with the knife that she used to cut the ends of the cigars—slash! slash!—Carmen started to cut the cross of Saint Andrew on the woman's face.

The case was obvious. I grabbed Carmen by the arm and politely said, "Sister, you'll have to come with us."

For an instant she stared at me in recognition, but then, with a certain air of resignation, said, "All right, then, let's get out of here. Where's my mantilla?" Placing the cloth on her head so that just one of her big eyes was showing, like a gentle lamb, she followed after my two men and me.

When we arrived at the guardhouse, the sergeant informed us that the incident involving Carmen was serious and ordered me to take her to prison. After placing a mounted soldier on either side of her, I walked behind Carmen as is customary for a corporal in such circumstances. Marching toward the city, the gypsy girl was quiet. However, when we arrived at the Sierpes (Serpent) Street—which as you are aware is so twisty that it deserves its name—she slowly and provocatively let her mantilla slip to her shoulder to reveal not only her shoulder but a slight smile on her face. Then, turning to me as inconspicuously as possible, she asked, "Officer, where are you taking me?"

"To prison, my poor child," I answered as kindly as I could and in the manner that a good soldier should address a prisoner, especially a woman.

"Aye, who knows what will become of me. Officer, please have pity on me. You're so young, so nice. . . ." Then, in a softer tone of voice, "Let me escape," she whispered. "Do it and I'll give you a piece of the *bar lachi,* which is a charm that will cause all women to love you." The *bar lachi,* señor, is a lodestone, which when used by a cunning gypsy can cast any number of spells. Scrape a little into a glass of white wine, and any woman who drinks it can no longer resist your advances.

"This is not the time to talk such foolishness," I answered as severely as I could. "I have my orders to take you to prison, and there is nothing we can do about it."

"Laguna ene bihotsarena—passion of my heart," she said to me suddenly in Basque, "are you from the Basque country?"

We Basques have an accent that is easily distinguishable from that of other Spaniards, as I'm sure you're aware, señor. On the other hand, there isn't one of them who can even learn to say *"Bai, jaona,"* meaning "Yes, sir." Carmen, therefore, had little difficulty guessing where I was from. You must know that since gypsies have no country of their own and are continually traveling, they speak all languages.

They're just as at home in Portugal or France as they are in Navarra and Catalonia—they are able to communicate with everyone, from Englishmen to Moors. Consequently, Carmen spoke Basque quite well. Our language, señor, is so lovely that it thrills us all the more to hear it spoken away from home. When it's time for my execution, I'd like a father confessor from my part of the country. But back to my story. Very touched to hear Carmen speak my language, I answered her in Basque, "I'm from Elizando."

"I'm from Etchalar," she said (which is only four hours from my home). "Some gypsies kidnaped and brought me here to Sevilla. I only work in the tobacco factory to try to earn enough money to be able to go home to be with my poor mother. She has no financial support but me and the cider from her tiny orchard of twenty apple trees. Aye, I would give anything to be back in the Basque country surrounded by snow-covered mountains. Here they've insulted me because I'm not from this land of thieves and vendors of rotten oranges. These awful women, sir, are all against me because I told them that their rude knife-carrying Sevillanos would be no match for just one of our brave boys from home with his blue beret and his *maquila* staff. Dear friend, won't you do something for a fellow countrywoman?"

Señor, she was lying. She has always lied. In her whole life I doubt if she ever spoke a word of truth. But as I listened to her, she convinced me—I couldn't help myself even though her eyes, mouth, and bronze skin gave her away as being a gypsy. On top of this, her Basque was dreadful, but still I believed she was from Navarra. I was so insane that I was ready to accept anything she said as truth. I thought that if some Sevillanos had insulted the Basque country, I would have felt like slashing their faces just as Carmen had done. In short, I was like a drunken man, saying silly things, and even worse, I was close to behaving like a complete fool.

"My countryman," she continued in Basque, "if I were to give you a shove and you fell down, I can guarantee that these two Castilian draftees couldn't hold me."

I swear to God I forgot all about my orders and everything else when I told her, "Well, my dear countrywoman, try it, and may Our Lady of the Mountain help you."

As chance would have it, at that very instant we were passing one of the many narrow twisted streets in Sevilla; Carmen swung around with all of her strength and punched me in the chest. I allowed myself to fall over backward and in one leap she was over me and running down the street, her skirt flying to show us her pretty legs. I had thought Basque girls were the only ones with lovely legs, but Carmen's (as fast as they were shapely) were certainly equal to anything I had ever seen. I leaped to my feet and, as I did so, placed my lance crosswise. It blocked the street for an instant and stopped my men as they tried to run after her. Then I started to give chase and they joined in behind me. Oh, but to catch her was like trying to capture the wind. Burdened down with our sabers, our lances, and our spurs, we didn't have a chance. In less time than it's taken to tell you about it, my prisoner had vanished, helped by all the neighborhood women who gave my men wrong directions and laughed at us. After searching up and down the street, we finally had to return to the guardhouse not only without Carmen but worse, without a receipt from the jail warden stating we had handed over our prisoner.

When interrogated, my men, in order not to be punished, revealed not only that Carmen had spoken Basque to me but that it didn't make sense for a punch from such a slight girl to knock over a big strong man. What had happened was embarrassingly obvious. Thus it was no surprise that at the end of the changing of the next guard I was not only stripped of my rank but sent to prison for a month. This was the first disciplinary action taken against me since I had joined the army, and needless to say, my long-awaited sergeant's stripes became no more than a dream.

Those first days in jail I was terribly depressed. When I joined the army, I was sure that one day at least I would become an officer. Two of my fellow Basques, Longa and Mina, are now captains-general. It made me sick to think that I had served such a long time and maintained such a good record and now it was lost. "With this black mark against me, I'll have to work ten times harder than when I was a recruit," I said to myself, "and I'll never get back in the good graces of my superior officers. So why did I do something so foolish, aware of what the punishment might be? It was all because of that gypsy whore who has made an ass of me and who right now is probably busy stealing something." Señor, it's hard to believe, isn't it? Even worse, I couldn't forget the sight of that brown skin that showed through her torn stockings as she ran away from us. In prison I stared through the bars at all the women going by, but not one of them could compare to that devil of a girl. You'll know that I was completely possessed when I tell you I couldn't keep myself from continually smelling the acacia flower she had tossed me and which, though withered, continued to make me heady with its fragrance. If witches exist, señor, that girl certainly was one!

One day the jailer brought me a loaf of the famous bread from the nearby village of Alcalá. "Your cousin sent you this," he said.

Very much surprised since I didn't have a cousin in Sevilla, I took the bread. "This is some kind of a mistake," I thought as I stared at the loaf. However, it looked so delicious and had such a fresh aroma that without hesitating to question for whom it was meant, I decided to eat a piece of it right then. As my knife cut through the crust it struck something hard. Examining the loaf more carefully, I found that someone had slipped a small English file into the dough before it was baked. Also hidden in it was a two-piaster gold coin. It was, without a doubt, a gift from Carmen. For gypsies like her, freedom is everything. They would burn down an entire town rather than spend one day in jail. This showed just how clever Carmen was, and I could imagine her laughing as she handed the jailer her loaf of bread.

With that little file I knew that it would not take more than an hour to saw through the thickest of the prison bars, and with the two-piaster gold coin I could buy some civilian clothes and get rid of my prison uniform. Climbing through the window and down the thirty-odd feet to the street didn't faze me, for as a young man I had often scaled cliffs to take eaglets from their nests—but something held me back. I didn't want to escape. My sense of honor as a soldier was still

very strong and deserting seemed the most shameful of crimes. But the fact that Carmen had remembered me and wanted to help me touched me deeply. When a man is in prison, it's wonderful to think he has someone on the outside who cares about him. To receive a gold coin from a woman embarrassed me and my immediate reaction was to return it, but where was I to find its true owner? Thus the file and coin remained hidden and were never used.

Following the ceremony of being demoted, I felt there was nothing left for me to suffer—little did I know that a further humiliation awaited me. It happened when I was released from prison and ordered to stand guard as a lowly private. I was so embarrassed that I would almost have preferred to have been executed than to have to stand there every day and be seen by those who had known me as a corporal marching along at the head of his company.

I was assigned sentry duty at the door of the colonel who was a rich young playboy. There were always a lot of people at his house, not only young officers but also some women—"actresses," as the neighbors politely called them. From my point of view it seemed that the whole city had arranged to congregate at his door just to look at me.

One day the colonel's carriage pulled up, and when the coachman opened the door, who should step out before my very eyes but the gypsy girl. How she had changed! Now she sparkled like a shrine, all dressed up in gold and ribbons. Her dress glittered with spangles, as did her blue shoes, and she seemed to have flowers and braid all over her! In one hand she was carrying a Basque tambourine. Two other gypsies accompanied her, a young girl and an old woman. This did not surprise me, for gypsy entertainers are usually led by an old woman along with a male guitarist. It's common for rich people to hire such a group to entertain at their parties, to dance and sing as well as to do other not so musical things. As Carmen and I stared at each other in recognition, I wished I were buried a hundred feet underground.

"Agur laguna—good morning," she said. "Officer, you're standing guard like a draftee!" And before I could find words to answer, she had disappeared into the colonel's house.

The party was held on the patio, and in spite of the crowd, I could see everything that went on through the grille of the iron gate. My head was caught in the whirl of sounds from the castanets, the drum, the laughter and bravos. My straining eyes would now and then capture a glimpse of her head as she leaped to the beat of the drum. And my face flushed as I heard many of the officers flirting with her. The answers she gave them I couldn't hear, but what I do know is that from that day it was clear that I had fallen completely in love with her. My passion was such that I wanted to burst into the patio and plunge my saber deep into the bellies of all the young playboys who were flirting with her. This torture went on for more than an hour until the gypsies came out. As Carmen brushed by me, she looked into my eyes and whispered, "Paisano, when people love good fried food, they go to eat at Lillas Pastia's place in Triana." And as lightfooted as a fawn, she leaped into the carriage; the coachman whipped the mules, and the sounds of laughter and singing disappeared into the night.

It takes little imagination to predict that the first thing I did when I got off duty was to get a shave and dress up as though I were preparing myself for a parade—and head for Triana. Lillas Pastia, who is as black as an African, is the gypsy owner of an inn where many people go to eat fried fish; and it was there that Carmen now lived.

As soon as she saw me her first words were "Come on, *paisano,* let's get out of here." Then she looked over her shoulder at Lillas and said, "I'm finished for the day. *Mañana será otro día.*" And no sooner had she drawn her mantilla over her face than we were out in the street going who knows where.

"Señorita," I said to her, "I think I have to thank you for the present you sent me in prison. The bread I ate. The file, which I use to sharpen my lance, I'll keep as a remembrance of you. But as for the money, here, take it."

"Well, what do you know; you haven't spent it," she exclaimed laughing. "I'm glad, for right now I'm broke. But who cares? A street dog like me never goes hungry. Come on, let's go out on the town. Let's throw it all away. You'll treat me."

We were on the road back to Sevilla, and at the beginning of Sierpes Street she bought a dozen oranges, which she made me wrap in my handkerchief. Accustomed to a strict military life, I suddenly felt like a schoolboy on vacation. As we walked along she also bought a loaf of bread, some sausage, and a bottle of manzanilla. Our last stop was a candy store where Carmen threw on the counter not only my gold piece but some coins she had in her own pocket. She then asked me to give her all my change—which embarrassed me since I was carrying very little money. It seemed that she wanted to buy the whole shop and spent every cent we had on the most expensive candies she could find. Along with our other packages, I had to carry these in paper bags.

Perhaps, señor, you know the place in Candilejo Street where there is a statue of King Pedro the Just. Well, I'm sure you're aware that the bust is there because it was on that spot that the king got into an argument with—and killed—an innocent young man. If I had only reflected more on that story and how that street ruined the life of that youth, I might have realized it held the same fate for me. We stopped in front of an old house where Carmen knocked on a door. It was opened by a gypsy woman with a face as evil as that of the devil's helper. When Carmen spoke in Romany, at first the woman, whose name was Dorothea, grumbled. But Carmen quieted her down by offering her two oranges, a piece of candy, and a taste of wine. Then, after putting a cloak around the old woman's shoulders, she led her out into the street.

When we were alone, Carmen bolted the door and began to dance and laugh as though she had gone crazy, singing, "Now I'm yours and you're mine. We can be *rom* and *romi*—gypsy man and wife." Not knowing what to do, I stood still in the middle of the room, loaded down with her purchases. Carmen grabbed them all from me and dropped them to the floor. Then she put her arms around my neck and whispered, "I pay my debts. I pay my debts. That's the law of the gypsies."

Aye, señor, what a day that was! What a day! Even when I think of it now, I feel I'm in heaven and I forget that the gallows awaits me tomorrow. We spent the whole day in that room, eating, drinking, and doing other things even more pleasurable. Like a little child she gulped down some of the candy, and then she stopped and said, "We should leave some for the old woman," upon which she stuffed an empty water jar full of sweets. There wasn't a trick she didn't know. She even smashed some of the pastries against the wall of the room, saying, "That's to attract the flies so they won't bother us." I told her I'd love to see her dance, but how could she without castanets? Did not having them stop Carmen? Not for a moment. She grabbed the old woman's only plate, broke it into two pieces—and began dancing for me, clacking together the fragments of crockery just as effectively as if they were made of ebony or ivory. A man could never be bored with that girl around—that's for certain!

Evening came and I heard the drums sounding retreat, calling me back to the barracks. "I have to get back to the barracks now for roll call," I told her.

"To your barracks?" she glared. "To your barracks! So you're really nothing but a black slave who like a sheep can be prodded about with a stick. So your character matches your yellow military uniform. You're not only a real canary, but a chicken-hearted one!"

I couldn't resist her. Though I knew I'd end up in the guardhouse, I spent all night with her. In the morning it was she who indicated I should go. "Listen to me, my little José, have I paid you back? Since you're not a gypsy, according to our law, I really owed you nothing. But you're so handsome and have given me pleasure. So we're even. Now, good-bye." I asked her when we could meet again. "When you're not such a sissy," she laughed.

Then, in a more serious tone of voice, she said, "Do you know what, *mi niño*? I think I'm a little in love with you. But that can't last. A sheepdog and a wolf can't get along together for very long. Maybe if you'd be willing to follow gypsy law, I'd be willing to be your woman. Aye, but what silly things I'm saying; this could never be. Believe me, *mi niño,* you're getting out of this very painlessly. You're not even aware that you've been with the devil today—the devil, you see, is not always black and evil-looking, and even though like a lamb I wear a woolen dress, I'm no sheep. Go and light a candle to the virgin who protects you, for today she's done her job. So leave while you're still able to do so. Now, for the last time, good-bye! Think no more of Carmencita or it'll be the end of you." She then unbolted the door, wrapped herself in her mantilla and disappeared into the street, leaving me standing alone in the room.

What she told me was the truth. Oh, how wise I would have been to erase her from my mind, but after that day in Candilejo Street she was all I thought about. From then on I spent all my free time roaming the city searching for her. I tried to pry news of her from old Dorothea and Lillas Pastia, but all they would say was that Carmen had gone to Portugal. It didn't take long, though, to find that they had both been lying, certainly instructed to do so by Carmen.

A few weeks after my rendezvous with Carmen on Candilejo

Street, I was assigned to stand sentry at one of the city gates alongside a hole that had been made in the wall by some smugglers. During the day workmen tried to repair the hole and at night a sentry was stationed there to prevent bandits from bringing in contraband. Often, before the sun went down, I'd see Lillas Pastia strolling back and forth near the guardhouse, talking to some of the other soldiers. All of them knew him and bought his fish and doughnuts. On one occasion he approached to ask if I had had any news of Carmen. "No," I told him.

"Well, you're sure to hear from her soon," he replied.

He wasn't mistaken. That night when I assumed my post at the smuggler's hole, as soon as the corporal had left me alone, a woman appeared out of the darkness. Immediately I knew in my heart that it was Carmen. Nevertheless, I ordered, "Get away from here! You can't pass!"

"Oh, don't be so mean," she answered, revealing her identity to me.

"What! So it's you, Carmen!" I replied, overwhelmed to see her after so many days of waiting for that moment.

"Yes, my *paisano*! Let's make this quick and to the point. Wouldn't you like to earn some pocket money? In a short while some people will be passing through this hole with packages. Don't stop them."

"No," I answered. "I have to keep them from passing through. Those are my orders."

"Your orders! Your orders! You didn't give much thought to them in Candilejo Street."

"Aye," I sighed, completely distraught by the mere thought of the day that Carmen had locked us in the room together. "Being with you was certainly worth forgetting my orders, but I can't accept money from smugglers."

"Let's see, then," she whispered. "If you don't want money, how would you like to celebrate with me again at old Dorothea's place?"

"No, I can't," I answered, nearly overwhelmed by my desire to say yes.

"So you're going to be difficult," she said. "If that's the way you want it, I know whom I'll ask. Your officer seems like such a nice fellow. I'll ask him if he wants to meet me at Dorothea's room, and he'll assign a sentinel like you to guard the door so that no one will bother us. *Adios,* canary; I'll really laugh the day you're sentenced to be hanged."

I couldn't help myself. I had to call her back and promise to allow every gypsy in the world to pass through the hole in the wall—if only she would reward me with what I desired. Immediately she promised to give herself to me the next day, and then ran to her friends who were waiting in the shadows. There were five of them, including Pastia, all loaded down with British merchandise. As they carried their smuggled goods through the hole, Carmen stood watch, ready to warn them of approaching soldiers with her castanets. However, the night was quiet and the smugglers rapidly finished their work.

The next day, as soon as I could, I went to Candilejo Street where Carmen kept me waiting for a long time. "I don't like people who have to be begged," she complained, obviously in a bad mood. "When we first met, you did me a great favor without asking for anything in return. Last night you bargained with me. Who knows why I'm even here now, because I don't love you anymore. So why don't you just go away. Here, take this money for your trouble." I felt like throwing the coin at her and slapping her face, but instead we argued for an hour before I furiously left her.

Like a madman I wandered aimlessly through Sevilla. Finally I entered a church where, sitting in the darkest corner, I wept like a child. Then a voice came from behind me, "Since you're a dragon, those must be dragon tears! How I'd like to brew them into a love potion." I dried my eyes and looked around. It was Carmen.

"Well, *paisano,* are you still angry with me?" she asked. "You know, even though I'm angry, I think I must be in love with you, for since you left me I've felt awful inside. And now I'm the one who's begging you to come with me to Candilejo Street."

Even though we made up then, Carmen's moods after that were like the weather. In the Basque country a storm is always nearest when the sun is shining brightest. After that second glorious meeting Carmen promised to see me the next day, but when I arrived Dorothea very courteously told me that Carmen had gone to Portugal "on gypsy business."

From past experience I knew I couldn't rely on Dorothea's words, so I began to look everywhere I thought Carmen might be. I must have gone up and down Candilejo Street a hundred times every day. One evening I stopped by Dorothea's place—I had bought the old woman so many glasses of anisette that I had almost won her over—when Carmen entered followed by a young lieutenant from my regiment.

"Get out of here right now!" she said to me in Basque. Dumbfounded, I stood there while my heart filled with rage.

"What are you doing here?" the lieutenant questioned me. "Move it! Get out of here at once and back to the barracks!"

I couldn't take a step. It was as though my legs were rooted to the floor. When the officer saw that I wasn't obeying and hadn't even taken off my cap, he became furious, grabbed me by the collar and shook me roughly. I can't remember what I said to him, but he drew his sword and I unsheathed mine. Suddenly Dorothea took hold of my arm and the lieutenant slashed me across the forehead. You see, señor, I still have the scar. Leaping backward, I threw the old woman to the floor. As the lieutenant lunged forward, I raised my sword and he ran himself through. Carmen immediately put the lamp out and told Dorothea to flee. As for me, I rushed into the street and began running without knowing where to go.

When at last I came to my senses and stopped, Carmen appeared. She hadn't abandoned me.

"You big stupid canary!" she hissed. "All you can do is make mistakes. Well, I predicted that I'd bring you bad luck. Now, don't just stand there; come with me. Let's get out of this mess. There's a solution for everything if you have a gypsy for a girlfriend. Give me that sword belt and tie this handkerchief around your head. Now wait for me in this alley, and I'll be back in a few minutes."

It seemed that Carmen had been gone only for a second when she returned with a striped cloak, which had come from who knows where. She made me remove my uniform and put on the cloak. Dressed in it and with the handkerchief she had used to bandage my bleeding forehead, I somewhat resembled the Valencian peasants who come to Sevilla to sell nut syrup. We crept to the end of the alley where she took me into a house that was quite similar to Dorothea's. Here she and another gypsy woman washed and dressed my wound better than any army surgeon could have done. Finally, after laying me on a mattress, they made me swallow some sort of liquid and I fell sound asleep.

Those women had certainly mixed some sort of sleeping potion into my drink, for I didn't wake up until late the next day. Because I had a terrible headache and a slight fever, it took me a while to recall the tragic scene that had taken place the night before. Carmen and her friend, both squatting on their heels beside my mattress, spoke in their gypsy tongue while they changed my bandages. Then both of them assured me not only that I would soon be completely well but that if I was caught in Sevilla, I would be shot on sight and that I had to escape as soon as possible.

"Mi niño," Carmen said, "because you can no longer be a soldier, the king will no longer feed you, so you'll have to earn your living in another way. It's time to think of a new career. You're not clever enough to be a pickpocket or shoplifter, but you're agile and strong. If you have the courage to do so, go away to the coast and be a smuggler. Didn't I promise you that I'd cause you to be hanged? Well, that's better than being shot. Anyhow, if you're good at smuggling, you'll live like a prince—if the civil guard doesn't catch you."

It was in this manner that that girl-devil described the new career she intended for me, the only one, frankly, that was left to me now that there was a price on my head. Because it seemed to me that I could be close to her by accepting such a life of danger and rebellion, it didn't take much for Carmen to persuade me to be a smuggler. From then on, I felt I could be sure of her love. In Andalucía I often heard people talk of smugglers who, musket in hand, rode good horses with their mistresses behind them. I could imagine myself galloping through the mountains with my lovely gypsy. However, when I spoke to her of our future life together, she rocked with laughter and told me that there is nothing so fine as a night spent in the mountains on a smuggling mission, when each man retires with his woman into their little tent made of blankets stretched over three bent branches.

"When I take you alone into the mountains with me," I told her, "I'll be sure of our love for there'll be no sharing you with lieutenants or anyone."

"Aye! So you're jealous," she replied. "So much the worse for you. How can it be that you're such an idiot when it comes to love? Since I've never taken any money to go to bed with you, isn't it obvious that I love you?"

When she talked that way I felt like strangling her. To make a long story short, Carmen found some civilian clothes for me and, dressed in them, I left Sevilla without being recognized. With a letter from Pastia, I set out for Jerez to see an anisette vendor at whose establishment smugglers used to meet. There I was introduced to a man nicknamed Dancairo who accepted me into his band. Soon thereafter we left for Gaucín, where Carmen had arranged to rendezvous with me. On these expeditions she served as spy for our band, and there never was a better one. When we met she had just returned from Gibraltar where she had arranged with a ship's skipper to haul some English merchandise up the coast where we'd be waiting for it. After we picked up our illegal cargo in Estepona, we hid a portion of it in the mountains and then, loaded down with the rest, made our way to Ronda. Carmen had gone there before us, and indicated when it was safe for us to enter the town. I was happy during those first trips. The life of a smuggler actually appealed to me more than that of a soldier. I had money and a mistress to whom I could afford to give gifts. I felt barely any remorse for the past and my new life for, as the gypsies say, "The pleasures in life distract one from the slight pain of a healing wound."

Everywhere we went we were well received. Even the other smugglers were nice to me. The fact that I had killed a man may have made many of them respect me. However, the most wonderful thing about my new life was that I was often with Carmen. She was more affectionate to me than ever; however, in front of the rest of the band she wouldn't admit to being my mistress, and she insisted that I make all kinds of promises that I wouldn't disclose any details about our intimate life. She had such power over me that I did everything she asked. My naïveté made me believe that her request for me to keep quiet about our love affair was a sign that she had the modesty of a decent woman. I was foolish enough to believe that she had given up her former ways.

Our band, which was made up of eight to ten men, hardly ever met except at decisive moments. Normally we were scattered in twos and threes throughout the mountain towns and villages. Each of us pretended to have a trade: One was a tinsmith, another a horse trader, and as for me, I sold clothing—although because of my trouble in Sevilla and my fear that I would be recognized, I hardly ever showed my face in big towns.

One day, or rather one night, when we met at the coastal village of Vejer, Dancairo seemed especially happy. "Now we're going to get one of our best men back," he told me. "Carmen has just played one of her cleverest tricks. She's helped her *rom* escape from the prison at Tarifa."

Since I had begun to understand the gypsy language, which most of the smugglers spoke, I was shocked by Dancairo's use of the word *rom*. "Her what? Her *rom*? Her husband?" I asked as I felt the blood drain from my face. "Then she's married!"

"Yes," replied Dancairo, "to García One Eye, a gypsy who's as crafty as she is. The poor fellow was sentenced to the gallows, but Carmen cast her spell over the prison surgeon so well that she was able to obtain freedom for her *rom*. Aye! That girl is worth her weight in gold. For two years she's been trying to arrange this escape. It seemed impossible until a new medical officer was assigned to the *presidio*. And Carmen did what she obviously does best to win him over.'' Señor, you can imagine how this affected me.

Not much time passed before I met García One Eye, who was without a doubt the most hideous monster ever born to a gypsy. If his skin was almost black, his soul was even darker. He was the wickedest scoundrel I've ever met. Carmen arrived at our camp with him and, when she called him her *rom,* you should have seen how she looked straight at me and then, when García glanced at her, she cringed. That night I was so furious that I didn't speak a word to her. In the morning, shortly after we had taken up camp, packed our mules, and started on the road, we looked over our shoulders and saw a dozen horsemen hot on our trail. It was a laugh to see the other members of our Andalusian gang looking so terrified after they had boasted they would gun down anyone who threatened us. There was general confusion with every man for himself—except Dancairo, García, a handsome young man from Esija named Remendado, and Carmen, who didn't lose their heads. The rest of the gang abandoned the mules and fled into the ravines where no one on horseback could follow.

Since we couldn't take our animals with us, we rapidly unloaded the most valuable of the loot onto our shoulders and tried to escape over the boulders and down the steepest slopes. Finally we had to throw our bundles before us and let them roll down the hill. Sliding on our heels, we followed them as best we could while trying to dodge our enemies' bullets. Even though a man in a woman's company in the face of danger wants to appear courageous, he should always remember that death doesn't play games. Although for the first time in my life I heard bullets whistling close to me, I wasn't in the least afraid. We all escaped except poor Remendado, who was shot in the back. I dropped my bundle and tried to carry him.

"Idiot!" García screamed at me. "What good is carrion to us? Finish him off and strip off his cotton stockings. I need a new pair."

"Drop him!" yelled Carmen. However, I didn't put him down until we reached the cover of a large boulder. But before I could pick him up again, García appeared behind me and fired point blank at our wounded companion's head.

"Now it would take a clever man to recognize him," said García as he looked down at the face that he had blown to bits.

That, señor, is an example of the kind of "fine" life that had become mine. By the time evening fell, we found ourselves in a dense thicket where, with nothing to eat and reduced to helplessness by the loss of our mules, we dropped with fatigue. Then what do you think that devil García did? As if nothing had happened he pulled out a pack of cards and, sitting next to the campfire, began to play with Dancairo. All this time I was stretched out on the grass, looking at the stars while reflecting on poor Remendado's death, feeling so miserable that I wished I were in his place. Not far from me crouched Carmen, now and then clicking her castanets as she hummed. Finally she came over to me and, pretending to whisper in my ear, kissed me two or three times before I could pull away.

"You're the devil in person," I told her.

"You're right," she answered.

Just before daybreak, Carmen set out for Gaucín; and once the sun had risen, a little goatherd arrived at our camp with some bread. We waited around all day for some word from Carmen and when evening came we moved close to Gaucín but still there was no sign of her.

At dawn, coming down the road, we sighted a pair of mules driven by a man who was accompanied by a well-dressed woman with a parasol and a little girl who appeared to be her maid.

"Those two mules and two women are gifts to us from Saint Nicholas," whispered García, smiling. "Four mules would have served us better, but never mind, we'll have to make do with these!" He grabbed his musket and cautiously moved down the path, taking cover in the undergrowth. Dancairo and I, following shortly behind, crept after him until we were within shooting distance. We leaped to our feet and ordered the mule driver to halt. When the woman saw us, instead of appearing frightened, she burst into laughter.

"Aye, what idiots!" she howled. "You took me for a lady." Carmen was so well disguised that only her voice revealed her identity. After jumping down from her mule and whispering for a moment with Dancairo and García, she said to me, "And for you, my little canary, we'll meet again before you're hanged. Now I'm off to Gibraltar on gypsy business, but you'll hear from me soon."

Once she had indicated where we could pitch camp without being discovered, she rode off on her mission. In all truth she was so clever that on many occasions she saved our necks. Before much time had passed Carmen sent some money and, of even greater value, the information that on a certain day and by a certain road two English lords, each carrying great sums of money, would be leaving Gibraltar for Granada. The appointed day arrived and the robbery went as planned. We not only took the Englishmen's money and their watches, but also their shirts; and they were lucky we didn't take their lives, for García wanted to murder them but Dancairo and I persuaded him not to.

Señor, if a man loses his head to a pretty girl, he can become a scoundrel without even meaning to. I had fought with the lieutenant and accidentally killed him for Carmen. This forced me to escape to the mountains. Once there, I went from being a smuggler to being a bandit before I knew it. After the incident with the English lords, we felt it was no longer safe to stay close to Gibraltar, so we set out again and took cover in the mountains around Ronda.

However, I should get back to my story. After much time had passed and we had had no word from Carmen, Dancairo wisely suggested, "One of us has to go to Gibraltar to find out what's going on. She must have something set up for us. I'd offer to go, but I'm too well known there."

"So am I," said García One Eye. "I've played too many tricks on those Englishmen who look like a bunch of lobsters in their red uniforms. And since I've got only one eye, I'm not an easy man to disguise."

Then came my turn to speak, and I was overjoyed at the possibility of being able to see Carmen and be alone with her again. "Then I guess it's left to me," I said. "Tell me what I have to do."

"Go either by boat or through San Roque, whichever you wish," they told me. "When you get to the port ask where a chocolate vendor called La Rollona lives, and she'll know how to find Carmen."

It was agreed that all three of us would ride to Gaucín where, disguised as a fruit vendor, I would leave García and Dancairo and set out for Gibraltar. In Ronda another bandit fixed up a false passport for me, and I was given a donkey loaded down with oranges and melons. When I arrived at Gibraltar I learned that although everyone knew about La Rollona, she was either dead or in prison. Her disappearance seemed to explain why Carmen had not been able to get messages to us. After stabling my donkey and loading myself down with oranges, I wandered through the town pretending to sell the fruit, all the time trying to catch a glimpse of a familiar face. Gibraltar is so full of scoundrels of all races that it seems like the Tower of Babel brought to life. You can't take ten steps in that place without hearing as many languages spoken. Although there were gypsies everywhere, I felt I couldn't trust any of them. While trying to determine if we were part of the same gang, I sounded them out and they sounded me out, each of us having no doubt, however, that we were fellow criminals.

During two days of walking aimlessly about, I'd learned nothing about either La Rollona or Carmen. At sunset, after I had done a little shopping and was strolling along thinking that it was time to return to Spain, I heard a woman's voice calling from a window above, "Orange vendor! Orange vendor!" Looking up I saw Carmen leaning over a balcony, and next to her was a curly-headed officer, who looked like an English lord, in a red uniform with golden epaulets. Carmen was extravagantly dressed, completely in silk with a shawl over her shoulders and a gold comb in her hair. As usual that shrewd girl, while acting out her comedy, couldn't contain her laughter. Speaking broken Spanish, the Englishman shouted for me to come up because the lady wanted some oranges. "Come on up," Carmen said to me in Basque, "and don't be surprised at anything you see."

To be truthful, nothing about her could have surprised me for she was capable of anything. Coming face to face with her again I don't know which I felt more strongly, happiness or rage. The door was opened by a tall English servant in a powdered wig, who led me into a magnificent salon where Carmen immediately ordered in Basque, "Don't speak a word of Spanish, and act as if you'd never seen me." Then turning to the Englishman, she said, "Don't you see, I was right. I knew he was a Basque, and now you're going to hear what a funny language he speaks. Look at that silly expression on his face, almost like that of a cat surprised in the larder."

"And you," I said to her in Basque, "you look like a common whore, and I'd like to slash your face in front of your lover!"

"My lover!" she exclaimed. "Come now! Tell me, did you figure that out all by yourself? It can't be—you mean you're really jealous of this imbecile? Why you're even a bigger fool than before our evenings in Candilejo Street. Thick-headed as you are, can't you see at this very moment how brilliantly I'm setting up this 'lobster'? This house is mine and soon all of his money will be mine, too. I lead him around by the nose, and I'll soon lead him to a place from which he'll never return."

"Now listen to me," I said, "if you ever do your gypsy business again so 'brilliantly,' as you put it, I'll take care of you so you'll never try it on anyone else!"

"Aye! Really now! Are you my *rom* to order me around? It's all right with One Eye, so what business is it of yours? You should be happy that you're the only man who can call himself my lover."

"What's that he's saying?" questioned the Englishman.

"That he's very thirsty and would like something to drink," answered Carmen, after which she fell back on the sofa and burst out laughing at her translation. Señor, when that girl laughed, there was no way to talk sense. Everyone laughed with her. Even the big Englishman was such an idiot that he began to laugh, and ordered the servant to bring me a drink.

While I was drinking, Carmen said to me, "See that ring he's wearing? If you want it, I'll give it to you."

"I'd give my finger to have your lord up in my mountains," I replied, "with each of us armed only with a *maquila*."

"*Maquila,* what does that mean?" asked the Englishman.

"*Maquila,*" said Carmen, knowing that it was one of our Basque iron-tipped staffs. "*Maquila,* that's an orange. Isn't that a very funny word for an orange? He says he'd like to have you eat one of his *maquilas.*"

"How nice," said the Englishman. "Then have him bring around some more *maquilas* tomorrow."

The servant entered while we were talking and said that dinner was served. Then the Englishman rose, gave me a coin, and offered Carmen his arm, as if she couldn't walk without his support.

"My boy, I can't invite you to dinner," Carmen said to me, "but tomorrow, just as soon as you hear the drum for the parade, come here with your oranges. You'll find a room that's far better furnished than the one in Candilejo Street, and you'll find out whether or not I'm still your Carmencita. And then we'll discuss gypsy business."

I didn't answer her, and when I was outside and in the street, the Englishman shouted down at me, "Bring some *maquilas* tomorrow!" And I could hear Carmen screeching with laughter.

I left without knowing what to do. That night I barely slept and, in the morning, I was so furious at the traitress that I made my mind up to leave Gibraltar without seeing her again. But at the first roll of the drum all my strength and decision left me. I grabbed my basket of oranges and ran to Carmen's place.

When I arrived there, I could see her big dark eyes watching me through the partially opened Venetian blinds. The servant in the powdered wig let me in at once. Then Carmen sent him off on an errand and, as soon as we were alone, broke into one of her silly fits of laughter as she threw her arms around my neck. Never had I seen her look so beautiful, dressed up like a madonna, perfumed, amid silk-covered furniture and embroidered curtains. Aye! And there I stood, dressed like the thief I was.

"My love," said Carmen, "I feel like smashing up everything here! I feel like setting fire to this house and running away to the mountains."

And then there were our caresses, our laughter. She danced until she tore the ruffles of her dress. Never did a she-monkey leap more wildly, make more grimaces, do more devilish tricks.

When her mood again became serious, she said, "Listen carefully. This is gypsy business. The Englishman believed me when I told him I want him to take me to Ronda to see my sister who's a nun." Carmen again rocked with laughter. "I'll make sure we ride by a place where you'll be waiting to attack and rob them of everything. We should probably kill him as well, but"—she paused for an instant with the same diabolical smile in her eyes that I had seen on other occasions—"but better yet, do you know what we should do? Arrange for One Eye to lead the attack! You bring up the rear. This English lobster is not only brave and a good shot, but he has two very accurate pistols. Do you understand what I'm trying to tell you?" She then interrupted herself with a ripple of laughter that made me shudder.

"I can't do that," I said, "even though I hate García. He's one of our gang. Maybe someday I'll get rid of him for you, but if that happens it'll be a clean fight. I'm not a gypsy by choice but by chance, and in most ways I'll always be a true and honorable Basque."

"You're a fool, a ninny, a real *payllo*—nongypsy!" she screamed. "You're like the dwarf who thought he was tall just because he could spit a long way. You don't love me! Now go away!"

When she told me to go away, I couldn't leave her. Instead I weakened once more and promised to return to the mountains and ambush the Englishman. In return, Carmen promised me that she'd play sick and wouldn't let the Englishman touch her until they left Gibraltar for Ronda. I stayed another two days in Gibraltar and she actually had the audacity to disguise herself and sneak over to the inn to be with me.

Upon returning to Spain I found Dancairo and García waiting in the mountains. We decided to spend the night in the forest and made a fire of pine cones, which blazed marvelously. With nothing else to do, I suggested to García that we play cards and he accepted. In the second game I became aware that he was cheating, and when I accused him of it and he began laughing, I threw my cards in his face. He tried to reach for his musket, but I put my foot on it and said, "I've heard that you're very good with a knife, in fact, that there's no one from here to Málaga better than you. Wouldn't you like to try your skill against me?"

Before Dancairo could separate us, I had hit García two or three times. Anger made him brave, and he pulled out his knife and I mine. Both of us told Dancairo to get out of the way and let us fight. Seeing that there was no way to stop us, he stood by silently. García was already bent over, crouching like a cat ready to spring. Knife thrust forward in his right hand, he held his hat in his left hand, Andalusian-style, in order to parry. As for me, I positioned myself in the Navarrese stance, directly in front of him, left arm raised, left foot forward,

and held my knife at thigh level. At that moment I felt the strength of a giant welling inside me. In a flash, he leaped at me and his knife slashed nothing but air. At that instant my blade found his throat, entering so deeply that I could feel his chin slide over my hand as I twisted so hard that the blade broke. In a second it was all over as the blade was forced out of the wound by a jet of blood as thick as your wrist. And García fell on his face, stiff as a board.

"What's gotten into you? What have you done?" Dancairo shouted.

"Listen, there was no way we could continue living together," I answered. "I love Carmen and I can't share her with anyone. Anyway, García was scum. I can never forget what he did to poor Remandado. Now there are only two of us, but we're good men. Come on, here you have me if you want me. I'll swear to be your friend for life."

"To the devil with love affairs!" exclaimed Dancairo as he extended his hand. "If you'd asked García for Carmen, he'd have sold her to you for a piaster. But now down to business. With only two of us left, how are we going to pull off this robbery tomorrow?"

"Let me do it all by myself," I replied joyously. "Now I feel I can take on the whole world." We buried García and pitched camp a short distance away.

The next day as we watched Carmen, her Englishman, their servant, and two muleteers come down the road, I said to Dancairo, "I'll deal with the Englishman. The others aren't armed; you frighten them away."

The Englishman was brave, and if Carmen hadn't pushed his arm when he fired, he would surely have killed me. And so it was that on that day I won Carmen back. The first thing I did was inform her that she was now a widow.

After I told her how I had killed García, she said, "You'll always be a fool. Too bad García didn't kill you. Your Basque way of fighting is a big joke—he's done away with better fighters than you. He's only dead because his time had come. Yours will come too!"

"And yours," I replied, "if you're not faithful to me."

"All right," she said. "More than once the coffee grounds at the bottom of my cup have shown that we'd end up together. Bah! But what must be must be!" And she clacked her castanets as she always did when she wanted to rid her mind of some unpleasant thought.

Señor, a man seems to forget everything when he's talking about himself. All of these details are surely boring you, but soon I'll be finished. After García's death, things went fairly smoothly between Carmen and me. Dancairo and I took into our gang some new men who were much more reliable than those from our original band, and we devoted all our time to smuggling. I have to admit that occasionally we robbed people traveling through the mountains, but we did that only when we were completely without money. Anyhow, we never harmed our victims and only stole their valuables.

Months passed and I was happy with Carmen. By arranging shipments of illegal goods for us to haul, she continued to be a tremendous help. Though she was in Málaga, or Córdoba or Granada, all it took was word from me, and she'd drop everything to come and meet me at some isolated inn or even at our camp. Only once did she upset me—when she was in Málaga where she met a rich merchant who soon became one of her victims. I was worried that to win his confidence she might give herself to him as she had with the Englishman in Gibraltar. Even though Dancairo tried every way possible to stop me, I went into Málaga in broad daylight, found Carmen, and brought her back to the camp where we had a violent quarrel.

It was then that she said to me, "Do you know what? Since you've become my *rom* for keeps, I love you less than when you were only my lover. I can't stand being pestered, and even worse, I won't put up with being bossed around. What I want is to be free to do what I please. Just be careful not to push me too far. Remember, if you bore me, I'll find someone better who'll get rid of you the way you got rid of One Eye."

Although Dancairo helped patch things up between us, neither of us would ever be able to forget the awful things we had said to each other. From then on our relationship was never the same. Shortly after that, some soldiers attacked us by surprise and not only killed three of our men, including Dancairo, but captured two others. As for me, I was seriously wounded and had it not been for the speed of my fine horse, I would have been caught by the soldiers. Completely exhausted, and with a bullet lodged in my body, I escaped into a dense forest. As I was getting off my horse I fell to the ground like a rabbit that has been shot with lead and is left to die in the underbrush. After one of the other survivors carried me into a cave, he rode off to find Carmen who was in Granada and who came to me at once.

For two weeks she wouldn't leave me for a moment. She didn't shut an eye in all that time. She nursed me back to health with a skill and devotion that I am sure not even the most loved man in the world has enjoyed from a woman. As soon as I was able to walk, Carmen made sure I was disguised enough not to be recognized and arrested and took me to Granada. Somehow, gypsy women have a way of finding safe places to hide, no matter where they are. Imagine, in Granada I spent more than six weeks in a house that was only two doors away from the home of the magistrate who was looking for me. Several times I stood behind our shutters and watched him walking by only a few feet away.

As I lay in pain day after day, I did a great deal of thinking and determined to change my way of life. I tried to convince Carmen that we should leave our pasts and Spain and go to America where we could try to live decent lives. But she only laughed at me and said, "Neither of us is made for planting cabbages. Our destiny in life, yours and mine, is to live at the expense of the *payllos*. Listen, I've made a deal in Gibraltar with Nathan ben-Joseph who has some cotton fabrics just lying there waiting for you to smuggle them into Spain. He knows that you're almost well and he's counting on you. What would our contacts in Gibraltar do if you didn't keep your word to them?" Once more I let her convince me and so it was that I returned to the sordid life of a smuggler.

While I was hiding out in Granada, Carmen attended some bullfights that were given there. And upon returning home, she spoke a good deal about a very talented picador called Lucas. Even though she knew the name of his horse and how much he had paid for his embroidered vest, I gave little thought at the time to her new and sudden interest. Then, a few days later, Juanito, the only other surviving member of the gang, told me he had seen Carmen and Lucas together at a store in Zacatín. It was only then that I began to get suspicious.

When I asked Carmen how she had become acquainted with the picador, she replied, "He's a young fellow who can be useful to us. Remember a stream is not moving unless you can hear the water splashing over the pebbles, and a man like Lucas does not have money unless he's skillful at something. Lucas has won twelve hundred reals in the corrida. That leaves us two choices: either get his money or, since he's a good horseman as well as quick-witted, let him join us. Two of our band are dead—you have to replace them. Take him with you."

"Neither he nor his money interests me," I replied, "and I forbid you to speak to him again."

"Be careful!" she snapped. "All it takes for me to do something is to have someone forbid me!"

Fortunately, the picador soon left for Málaga, and I was busy preparing to smuggle ben-Joseph's cotton fabric from Gibraltar into Spain. Both Carmen and I had to put a tremendous amount of work into this expedition, which may have been why, for the moment anyway, I—and perhaps she—forgot about Lucas.

Señor, it was just about this time in my story that I met you, first near Montilla, then later at Córdoba. I prefer not to talk about the second time, when I found you and Carmen alone together. Who knows what went on between you? What I do know, however, is that she not only stole your watch, but was also after your money and that ring you still wear on your finger. It was a magic ring, she told me, and she had to have it. After you left we had a violent quarrel, until I hit her and she grew pale and wept. I felt terrible, for it was the first time I had ever seen her cry. During the entire day she sulked even though I continually begged forgiveness. When I left Montilla she refused to kiss me good-bye.

For three days my heart was filled with sadness but finally she returned with a smile on her face and appeared as happy as a lark. It seemed that our quarrel had been completely forgotten, and we acted like a pair of lovers at the beginning of their affair. When it was time for us to part, Carmen said to me, "I'm going to the fiesta in Córdoba to find out who will be leaving there with money so I can tell you which ones to rob."

I allowed her to leave, but once I was alone, I began thinking about the fiesta and about Carmen's change in moods, from hating me a few days earlier to showing me so much affection now. "It must be she's somehow had her revenge," I thought to myself. "Otherwise, why would she come back to me so suddenly and make up?" As I was lost in these thoughts, a peasant passed by and told me that there was a bullfight in Córdoba. My blood began to boil and like a madman I got on my horse and rode straight to the bullring.

Once inside, I asked about Lucas, and when he was pointed out to me, I caught sight of Carmen nearby in a first row ringside seat. It took no more than that glance to confirm my suspicion.

When the first bull entered the ring, Lucas, as I had expected, revealed that he had a romantic interest in someone in the crowd. He grabbed the ribboned dart—the ranch's colors—from the bull's shoulder and presented it to Carmen who promptly put it in her hair.

Then the bull, as if answering my wish for revenge, knocked over both Lucas and his mount so that the man was pinned beneath the horse and the bull bore down on both of them. When I looked up to see how Carmen was reacting, her seat was empty. In that crowd it was impossible for me to find her, so I had to wait until the bullfight was over.

Then, señor, I went to the house where she had taken you and waited there until two in the morning when she returned, obviously startled to see me. "You're coming with me," I told her.

"Very well," she replied, "let's go."

When I had saddled my horse and was mounted, I pulled her up behind me and we rode through the night without exchanging a word. When we finally dismounted at dawn at an isolated inn close to a small hermitage, I broke the silence and said to Carmen, "Please listen to me! I'll forget everything. I'll never mention Lucas to you again, but promise me just one thing, that you'll come with me to America and that you'll live a respectable life there."

"Never," she said, sulking. "I won't go to America. I like it here."

"That's only because you're near Lucas," I answered. "But think it over. Even if he gets well, with his profession he won't live very long. Anyway, why should I have a grudge against him? I'm tired of killing all of your lovers. Next time you're the only one I'll kill."

"I've always thought you'd murder me," she said, staring at me with her wild eyes. "There have been signs along the way. The first time we met, a priest had just passed the door of my house. And tonight as we were riding out of Córdoba, didn't you notice anything? A rabbit darted across the path and between your horse's hooves. That's fate."

"Carmencita!" I pleaded. "Don't you love me anymore?" She didn't answer, sitting cross-legged on a reed mat and continuing to draw lines in the sand with her finger. "Carmen, let's change our way of life," I begged. "Let's go away and live someplace where we can always be together. You know, not far from here we've got a hundred and twenty ounces of gold buried under an oak, and apart from that, Nathan ben-Joseph is still holding some money for us."

"First I make you change your life and now you want me to change mine," she said and smiled. "I knew that it would have to happen that way."

"Think it over," I replied, "for both my patience and my courage have been pushed to their limit. Make up your mind, or else I'll make up mine!"

I left her and walked to the hermitage where I discovered a monk lost in prayer. How I, too, would have liked to be able to pray, but I couldn't. When the monk had finished and stood up, I went over to him. *"Padre,"* I asked, "will you pray for someone who is in grave danger?"

"I pray for all who are afflicted," he answered.

"Is it possible for you to say a mass for a soul that is perhaps soon going to appear before its maker?" I asked.

"Yes," he replied as his eyes intently scanned my face. Seeing that there was something strange in my expression, he attempted to make me talk. "Haven't I seen you before?" he asked.

I placed a piaster on his bench and asked, "When will you be saying mass?"

"The son of the innkeeper will come to serve it in a half hour," he answered. "But, young man, tell me, is there something on your conscience that's bothering you? Will you listen to the words of a Christian?"

I told him that I would return later and, close to tears, ran out of the hermitage. A short distance away I lay down on the grass and stayed there until I heard a bell that summoned me back to the chapel. I didn't enter, but remained outside until mass was over, and then returned to the inn with the hope that Carmen had fled. She could have taken my horse and ridden away—but I found her still there. She would have done anything not to give the impression that I had frightened her. While I was at the hermitage, she had unstitched the hem of her dress to remove some of the lead that weighted it down. After melting the metal, she had dropped it into a bowl of water and was now sitting looking into the water, trying to read the mystery of its contents. In fact, she was so absorbed in her magic that she wasn't even aware I had returned. She removed a piece of lead from the bowl and turned it slowly. Her face clouded with sadness as she studied it from every angle. Then she sang one of those magic songs that gypsy women use to speak to María Padilla, the Grand Queen of the Gypsies.

"Carmen, will you come with me now?" I asked. She rose to her feet, threw aside the wooden bowl, and put her mantilla over her head, ready to leave. My horse was saddled, she mounted behind me, and we rode away.

After we had traveled awhile, I asked her again, "Well, Carmen, you're willing to follow me now, aren't you?"

"Yes, I'll follow you even until death," she answered, "but never again will I live with you."

When we were in a lonely gorge and I reined up my horse, she asked, "Is this the place?" and with one leap was on the ground. She took off her mantilla and flung it to her feet. With one hand on her hip, standing completely still, she stared right into my soul and said, "I know you're going to kill me—that's my destiny—but you'll never make me give in."

"Be reasonable," I pleaded. "Listen to me. The past is all forgotten. You know that you were the ruin of me—because of you I became a bandit and a murderer. Carmen, my Carmen! Let me save you and myself with you!"

"José, what you're asking of me is impossible," she replied. "Don't you see, I no longer love you, and that's why you want to kill me. If I wished, it would be simple to tell you another lie, but I can't be bothered doing even that. Between us everything is over. As my *rom,* you have the right to kill me, your *romi,* but Carmen will always be free. She was born a gypsy and she'll die a gypsy."

"Then you're in love with Lucas?" I asked.

"Yes, I did love him as I loved you, but for less time perhaps. At this moment, however, I love nothing anymore, and I hate myself for having loved you!"

Throwing myself at her feet, I took hold of her hands, which became wet with my tears. I reminded her of all the happy moments we had spent together. I even offered to remain a bandit just to please her. Everything, señor, I offered her everything, if only she would love me again!

To my pleading, she replied, "Love you again? That's possible. Live with you again? Never!"

Suddenly I was completely overcome with the wildest fit of rage. When I took my knife in my hand, I would have given anything to see her look afraid and beg me for mercy—but that woman was a devil. It was then that I shouted, "For the last time, will you live with me?"

"No! No! Never!" she said, angrily stamping her foot as she pulled from her finger a ring I had given her and threw it into the underbrush.

I stabbed her twice, using the knife I had taken from One Eye after breaking my own blade in his throat. With the second blow, Carmen fell without a whimper. I think that I can still see her big black eyes looking at me in a fixed stare before they clouded over and closed. Overcome with grief I lay down next to her body and stayed there for more than an hour. When I came to my senses I remembered that Carmen had often told me she wanted to be buried in a forest, so with my knife I dug a grave for her there and laid her in it. After searching for a long time, I found her ring and placed it and a little cross beside her in the grave. Then I got on my horse and galloped toward Córdoba where I turned myself in at the first guardhouse. I confessed that I had killed Carmen, but I wouldn't disclose where I had buried her. The monk from the hermitage prayed for her. He said a mass for her soul. Poor Carmen! The gypsies are to blame. If they hadn't brought her up to have their evil ways, she might be alive right now.

THE *CARMEN* OF SEVILLA—
AFTER THE NOVEL

BIZET AND *CARMEN*

A Parisian like Mérimée, Georges Bizet was born on October 25, 1838. His musical aptitude was so stunning that by the time he was nine years old he was accepted as a pupil at the Paris Conservatory. At the age of nineteen he had not only written his first opera, *Le Docteur Miracle,* a one-act comedy, but had also won a Prix de Rome. After completing studies in Italy, Bizet returned to Paris intent on writing music for the stage.

His next three works, *Les Pêcheurs de Perles* (1863), *La Jolie Fille de Perth* (1867), and *Djamileh* were very coolly received by the critics. Five years after marrying Geneviève Halévy, the daughter of one of his former teachers, Bizet in 1872 wrote the incidental music for Alphonse Daudet's *L' Arlésienne* and enjoyed his first—and last—taste of fame. After the failure of *Djamileh,* the success of *L' Arlésienne* gave him the confidence to create *Carmen.* "I am absolutely certain," he wrote, "that I have found my way; I know what I am doing."

So inspired was Bizet by Mérimée's novel and so confident of his ability to translate it into opera that he remarked, "People make me out to be obscure, complicated, tedious, more fitted by technical skill than lit by inspiration. Well, this time I have written a work that is all clarity and vivacity, full of color and melody. It will be entertaining. . . ." However, his librettists, Henri Meilhac and Ludovic Halévy (his wife's cousin), did not share this enthusiasm. Before *Carmen* was finished, Halévy commented, "This little thing has little importance for Meilhac and me."

Nicholas John tells us: "The two librettists tried to soften the aspects of Bizet's chosen subject which might cause offense. Their collaboration, which lasted over twenty years, was notorious for their texts of Offenbach's satirical operettas, which were certainly not performed at the Opéra-Comique. While *Carmen* was in rehearsal between October and December 1874, they had not less than four other works staged in Paris. Meilhac was a playwright, with little interest in music, who supplied the dialogue and comic relief. Halévy, the nephew of Bizet's teacher and father-in-law, the opera composer Fromental Halévy, wrote the verse. Their published text of *Carmen* differs considerably from what Bizet set to music. They continually proposed refrains and rhyming couplets which would have been ideal for conventional opéra-comique, or indeed for Offenbach's routines, and Bizet 'ferociously' altered and rejected them."

"The librettists," write Nell and John Moody, "in cutting Mérimée's novel to opera length had to leave out much illuminating detail. This, followed later by careless translations and drastic cutting of the published dialogue, has often made definition of the characters in the opera inadequate and in fact downright wrong. Both Carmen and Don José have often suffered from this.

"As is so clear from Mérimée, they are a pair of absolute opposites, fatally attracted to each other. To José, Carmen has all the things he lacks: a total lack of inhibition, irresponsibility in personal relationships and an infinite capacity for enjoying life. To her, José is equally fascinating: a gentleman, with looks, and an elegant detachment, who does not chase every girl who comes his way, yet is obviously a passionate, if a rather buttoned-up, young man, whom it would be a pleasure to unbutton.

"According to the book, to which the operatic characterization is faithful, Carmen was small, slim, young, 'prettier than any gipsy,' with eyes that had a sensual yet savage look with a wolfish glint. She wore her clothes beautifully and was a professional dancer at parties. Because she could not afford scent, she wore heavily scented flowers, acacia in the day and jasmine by night. She 'munched sweets like a child of six,' was always laughing, sending people up, with a lovely sense of the ridiculous; yet able to cope with any situation. She was more than faithful to her own people. She obeyed gipsy law: she paid her debts—to José in kind for freeing her from Prison. José exasperated her by his possessiveness—'dog and wolf don't mate for long' . . . 'I must be *free* to do as I like,' but when he was wounded or ill she would nurse him night and day devotedly. At the end she goes to him deliberately, knowing he may kill her, yet she will not surrender to him: she must be free. Basically a really heroic character.

"José is a proud Basque gentleman, a Don of a very old family; stalwart, good-looking, and of a very passionate nature although inhibited by his upbringing. He was being trained, in the family tradition, to go into the Church. But his studies came second to his love of sport. One day after a game of Pelota, his opponent picked a quarrel with him. José's terrific temper suddenly blazed, the boy was killed, José had to leave the country. He joined the army and soon became a corporal. On three other occasions in the opera we see his temper blaze. In Act Two, when his officer slaps his face, he would have killed him; in Act Three when he fights Escamillo [who replaces Lucas in the opera]; and at the end, when Carmen throws his ring at him, it suddenly blazes again and he has killed her before he knows what he has done.

"Subconsciously he can never escape from his family morality; his duty as a son, as a soldier, his feeling that marriage must be for life. When he returns to the bullring in the last scene to find Carmen, his only instinct is to 'save' her, to take her away to start a new life. Both are heroic in their different ways: in spite of the degradation José has suffered through Carmen, his love for her is as strong as ever. The tragedy is that they should ever have met."

Michel Raboud makes an interesting observation when he says, "One of the structural features of the opera, which did not appear in Mérimée's short story and which accounts for a number of transformations in the libretto, is the defeat of sentimental love by vital passion. Rather than the weak soldier who renounces his duties to follow a dangerous seducer (which is how he too often appears), Bizet's Don José is a man whose fatal vocation compels him to abandon a pale sentimental love and banal occupations, and to plunge into what he does not know—the outlaw world of passion. Like Des Grieux when meeting Manon in Prévost's novel, Don José begins to live when he meets Carmen: love acts as a second birth, transforming a rather ectoplasmic character into a full-blooded man. One could argue that if he shows weakness it is not by following Carmen, but by being unable to follow her completely. He returns to his dying mother instead of responding to Carmen's vital challenge: he is not a free man and he loses her."

Meilhac and Halévy add characters and incidents to their libretto that are not found in Mérimée. Most important of these are Micaela, Don José's childhood, peasant sweetheart who brings news to him of his dying mother, and Escamillo, the matador who replaces the picador Lucas from the novel. Other characters who appear in the opera and not in Mérimée are Zuniga, a captain; Morales, a brigadier; Frasquita and Mercedes, Carmen's gypsy friends. On the other hand, several of Mérimée's characters have gotten lost on the way to the opera: Longo, Mina, and, most important, García One Eye. Carmen's death, as Mérimée describes it, takes place in the open country, far from her new lover, Lucas; in the opera Don José kills her outside of the Sevilla bullring where the crowd is heard cheering Escamillo's triumph. Also absent from the stage version are Don José's pleas to Carmen to go with him to America and start a new life.

Micaela and Escamillo were very cleverly created to serve as foils for Carmen and Don José. Michel Raboud tells us: "The introduction of Micaela into the opera becomes a necessity. She represents Christianity, family bonds, legality and sentimental love, all to be broken down by the eruption of passion. She shares with Don José a musical vocabulary of tender and intense lyricism, which is utterly antithetic to Carmen's songs and dances."

"Micaela," write Nell and John Moody, "often played as a nonentity, was Halévy's invention, thought up to sweeten the 'disgusting' Carmen pill for the disapproving management. But the text, and Bizet's treatment of it, created a rounded character. She was brought up by José's mother, as a daughter of a good family, fit to marry the son and heir. She has a strength that can challenge Carmen, and a wit that can deal with soldiery or smugglers.

"There is much else in Mérimée's novel about the characters which can help us to understand them. It is compulsive reading. No wonder Bizet wanted to set it!"

"The character of Escamillo," says Michel Raboud, "is the other main addition in the opera to Mérimée's story. He is an incarnation of sheer virility, and Bizet reveals this otherwise subdued aspect of Don José's character by giving the two men a carefully balanced quarreling duet: by eventually defeating the toreador, Don José displays the seriousness of his passion and his skill as a fighter. But although Carmen leaves Don José for Escamillo, it does not follow that the two men are rivals of comparable stature. Escamillo's love is gallantry of a kind similar to that which Carmen lightheartedly rebuked in Zuniga. He is ready to wait for his turn in Carmen's favours, without showing too much impatience. . . . If he appeals to Carmen, despite his shallow vanity, it is because he is on familiar terms with death: the first thing he offers her is 'to pronounce her name the next time he kills a bull.' He freely risks his life with every bull he fights and freedom is indeed her strongest passion."

But it is Carmen alone who is the force behind both Mérimée and Bizet, and her complexities are what intrigue us. Michel Raboud comments:

"The enduring mystery and fascination of Carmen is due to the fact that we are never given the least psychological clue to the deep motives of her actions and the hierarchy of her feelings. She does not comment on herself; she only states repeatedly her unyielding will to remain free. Does she love Don José? She never says so, otherwise than elusively and playfully, and she never attempts, as Massenet's Manon constantly does, to give reasons for her behaviour. Nevertheless, she does choose him, by throwing him a flower in the first act, presumably because he is different from other men: he alone does not even look at her. The music which immediately precedes her gesture, her 'fate' theme ending on a long silence after a suspended single note, obviously refuses to comment on her feelings—Fate has made its entrance, sudden and unexplained. She is disappointed several times by Don José's indecisiveness, and mocks him sharply. But she is intrigued by a man for whom love is not a game, and who is deadly serious about it. Indeed it is death she finally challenges by accepting, despite all warnings, to meet Don José. And she also knows it is worth missing the *fiesta,* over which she was to reign, in order to have this confrontation.

"Such a provocative attitude is not disguised suicide, not an idealistic attempt to sublimate her love, but something rationally absurd she simply *has* to do to remain herself. In this respect Carmen's death is radically different from that of Isolde whose radiant joy in death comes from her mystical belief that eternal love will transcend it. Both she and Tristan are conceived as passive *victims* of love and death, whereas Carmen and Don José act their love and death until the end. By killing her—and not Escamillo, which would seem at first glance more rational—Don José fulfills a need to possess her. But confronting him with courage, Carmen proclaims her free will and firmly asserts her ego; she *deliberately* chooses to accomplish her destiny. This is what Nietzsche considered essentially tragic: to face death not in an idealist's *refusal* of life, but in a full, if paradoxical, *assent* to it."

Bizet, in part, created the preproduction problems that plagued *Carmen* by writing grand opera for the Paris Opéra-Comique, which was accustomed to light comedy. To present a tragedy in which a brazen seductress is stabbed to death by her lover on a set full of gypsies, prostitutes (the audience was appalled to see women smoking on stage), and smugglers was akin to showing *A Streetcar Named Desire* at a theater whose standard matinee repertoire was Doris Day films. But even the problems of trying to get *Carmen* to her opening night were many.

Ellen Bieler tells us:

"The composition of *Carmen* was filled with difficulties. The management of the Paris Opéra-Comique, which had commissioned the work, were violently opposed to the opera's mélange of Gypsies, prostitutes, murderers and thieves. They protested that the Opéra-Comique was a family theatre, catering to the bourgeoisie. The singer who was first approached to create the title role rejected it as 'scabrous.' Because the management could not afford to pay the singers top-rank salaries, negotiations continued interminably with Marie Galli-Marié, the mezzo-soprano next approached to sing the part of Carmen. Rehearsals were often postponed because of lack of cash.

"As rehearsals progressed, the Opéra-Comique's management worried more and more about 'repercussions' and urged that the opera's ending be changed to a happy one. Even Bizet's librettists, Ludovic Halévy and Henri Meilhac, pressed the toreador to stop chucking chorus girls under the chin and tried to persuade Galli-Marié to interpret Carmen in a more restrained, more refined manner. In the latter endeavor they were unsuccessful, for Galli-Marié was artist enough to recognize the necessities of the story. Mysterious comments began to appear in newspaper, saying that the Opéra-Comique could no longer be considered a family theatre if Carmen were performed. Several hours before the premiere, the government awarded Bizet the Legion of Honor—why, no one now knows, although contemporary wit said, 'Because it won't be possible to decorate him after Carmen hits the stage.'

"There were also musical difficulties in preparing the opera. Members of the chorus, accustomed to enter in a body, assume statuesque poses and point their voices at a particular place, complained that they could not conceivably sing if they had to enter as individuals and move around the stage. The theatre's director did not like the music and called it Indochinese music. Galli-Marié did not like the way Bizet had written the 'Habanera.' Bizet obligingly rewrote it thirteen times, then gave up in despair and adapted what he thought was a Spanish folk song. This music pleased Galli-Marié. Escamillo felt that his big aria was unworthy of him. Bizet, muttering, 'They want ordure and they'll get it,' removed the offending aria and wrote in the present toreador bombast. And the orchestra had to be led by the nose through the strange music.

"The premiere of Carmen took place at the Opéra-Comique on March 3, 1875. The audience included most of the Parisian musical world and was not unfriendly, though it was not exactly enthusiastic either.

"The performance itself was mediocre. Galli-Marié was excellent, although her interpretation was considered scandalous. The tenor had trouble maintaining his pitch. A tympanist miscounted measures and thumped enthusiastically in the middle of the duet between José and Carmen. The chorus could not manage Bizet's rhythms, and the cigarette girls, unaccustomed to the cigarettes they carried, gasped and choked through their most important piece. The stagehands also seemed to have trouble, since the first intermission lasted twenty-three minutes, the second forty-two and the third again twenty-three. The opera's first act received enthusiastic applause; the second was applauded mildly; the third less, the fourth none.

"The press was incredibly savage to Carmen. Reviewer after reviewer either sneered at the music or hysterically denounced the libretto's immorality. Oddly enough, though they attacked the premiere outrageously, a few years later the same critics praised Carmen as lavishly as they had damned it before.

"Carmen languished on at the Opéra-Comique through the spring of 1876; it was discontinued in May of that year and briefly revived in November. All in all, it had forty-six performances before gradually diminishing audiences."

PLOT SUMMARY OF *CARMEN*

Act One: A public square in Sevilla, the time, 1820. It is noon and soldiers, watching people pass, stand around a guardhouse. Across the plaza is the tobacco factory. At this moment Micaela, a shy young country girl, arrives and asks for information about Don José, whom she has loved since childhood, and the soldiers try to flirt with her. When the officer on duty, Morales, tells her that Don José will be there after the next guard change, she leaves, saying that she will return.

The relief arrives led by Lieutenant Zuniga, and when Morales tells them about Micaela, Corporal José realizes that the girl he speaks of is an orphan whom his mother had raised and taken care of. The lieutenant, however, new to Sevilla, has his mind on other things—the girls at the tobacco factory.

When the bells ring noon and the girls return to the factory, the square is full of young men waiting to flirt with them. Carmen appears with a flower between her teeth, and ignores all of the men's advances. Only José, who pays no attention to her, attracts her interest and she throws the flower in his face, leaving him embarrassed and confused while everyone laughs.

As the square empties and José reflects on what the wild and beautiful Carmen has just done, Micaela appears and gives him a letter from his mother in which she asks him to marry its bearer. After Micaela leaves, a tremendous uproar explodes from the tobacco factory as the cigarette girls rush into the square screaming that Carmen has stabbed a fellow worker. Lieutenant Zuniga orders José to investigate and when he returns with Carmen she not only refuses to be interrogated, but also tries to attack one of the other girls. The lieutenant then orders José to take her to prison. Once they are alone, Carmen urges José to release her, and sings about the fun that can be had at Lillas Pastia's café across the river, also indicating that if he helps her, she might just make him her lover. Now caught in her web, José agrees, and as they move through the streets of Sevilla, he allows Carmen to escape. For this he is reduced in rank and sent to prison.

Act Two: The setting is the tavern of Lillas Pastia near the banks of the Guadalquivir River, presumably in Triana as in the novella. The place is full of smugglers and other "lowlifes" along with some soldiers who are being entertained by gypsy girls, including Carmen. Lieutenant Zuniga, who is with the soldiers, tells Carmen, while flirting with her, that José has just been released from prison. In truth, Carmen has been waiting at Lillas Pastia's for days for this very moment so that she can repay the man who went to jail for her. As the night passes, the famous matador Escamillo and his entourage arrive. The officer invites the bullfighter to have a drink and toast with them. Escamillo sees Carmen and is so strongly attracted to her that he asks her to join him. Although she refuses, she does so in such a way that we know her refusal is only temporary.

Later, when the tavern is empty, the leader of the gypsy smuggling band, El Dancairo, and one of his gang, Remendado, along with Mercedes and Frasquita, two of Carmen's gypsy friends, try to persuade Carmen to join them on a smuggling expedition. She has vowed, however, to wait for José, who soon arrives. Once they are alone, Carmen does her wildest and most seductive dance, hoping to fascinate the stolid soldier into joining the band of smugglers. A distant bugle sounds retreat, warning José that he must leave immediately or be arrested as a deserter. He says he must go, but Carmen persists. When he refuses to stay, she becomes furious even though he shows her the flower she had thrown at him, which he has carefully saved, and confesses his love for her. Determined, Carmen declares that if he loved her he would follow her to the mountains, but José remains firm in his refusal.

At this moment his lieutenant, Zuniga, enters, having come back to the tavern for Carmen, and orders José to return to the barracks. José disobeys and the two men begin a fight, which is broken up by the gypsy smugglers. They restrain the lieutenant, and José, having struck an officer, now has no choice but to join the gypsies and Carmen.

Act Three: The setting is a mountain pass, presumably near Ronda, where the smugglers have stopped to rest. Although José is still very much in love with Carmen, she is becoming bored with him and tells him to return to his mother. They quarrel and he says that he will kill her rather than lose her.

When Frasquita and Mercedes deal out cards to read their fortunes, Carmen joins in, and repeatedly deals herself death.

It is decided that José will stay behind while the women and other male members of the band go on a smuggling mission. Shortly after they have left, Micaela is seen (out of sight of the others) praying for protection. When she has finished her prayer, the matador Escamillo arrives at the gypsy camp. He was buying bulls on a neighboring ranch when he learned that Carmen was nearby and he is trying to find her. He meets José, not realizing who he is, and tells him of his search for the gypsy girl. José then reveals his identity and they begin to fight. Just when José is about to kill Escamillo, Carmen and the smugglers appear to separate them and save the matador's life. Before Escamillo leaves, he invites Carmen and the other smugglers to attend one of his corridas in Sevilla.

Once Escamillo is gone, one of the gypsies discovers Micaela hiding nearby. Micaela begs José to return to his mother, but because of his love for Carmen he refuses, even though all the gypsies encourage him to go. Just when he is about to send Micaela off alone, she tells him that his mother is dying. Only then does he agree to leave, but not without telling Carmen that he will be back for her. Carmen, however, is now more interested in Escamillo, whose song is heard in the distance.

Act Four: Outside the Sevilla bullring, Carmen, now Escamillo's lover, arrives to see him fight, along with Frasquita and Mercedes, who soon see José lurking in the crowd. They try to warn Carmen but, certain of her fate, she goes to confront him. Miserable and dishonored, José begs her to return to him and even offers to rejoin the smugglers' band if only she will do so. Unmoved by his pleas and threats, Carmen shows that their affair has really ended by removing from her finger a ring he had given her and throwing it at him. At that moment José pulls out his knife and stabs her. Just as the triumphant Escamillo appears, José drops to the ground beside Carmen's still body and addresses a few last words to her before calling for the soldiers to arrest him.

CARMEN

Opera in Four Acts

Music by

Georges Bizet

Words by

H. MEILHAC and L. HALÉVY

English Version
by
RUTH and THOMAS MARTIN

CAST OF CHARACTERS

MORALES, an officer . . . . Bass

MICAELA, a peasant girl . . . . Soprano

ZUNIGA, a lieutenant of dragoons . . . . Bass

DON JOSÉ, a corporal of dragoons . . . . Tenor

CARMEN, a gypsy girl . . . . Soprano

MERCEDES } gypsy companions of Carmen { Mezzo-Soprano
FRASQUITA } { Mezzo-Soprano

ESCAMILLO, a toreador . . . . Baritone

EL REMENDADO } smugglers { Tenor
EL DANCAIRO } { Baritone

Cigarette Girls, Dragoons, an Innkeeper, Smugglers, Dancers

PLACE: In and near Seville
TIME: About 1820

G. SCHIRMER
New York/London

SYNOPSIS OF SCENES

ACT I

No. 1 Prelude

No. 2 Scene and Chorus

(*A square in Seville. On the right, the door of a tobacco factory; on the left, a guardhouse; at the back, a bridge. When the curtain rises, Corporal Morales and the soldiers are grouped in front of the guardhouse. People are coming and going on the square.*)

CHORUS OF DRAGOONS
Lazy people, crazy people,
Old and young, bold and shy;
Strolling along or hustling by,
Nobody knows the reason why.
Neither do I!

MORALES (*nonchalantly*)
Lolling idly about and smoking,
Playing dice and cards,
We pass the time in talk and joking
With our fellow guards.
Lazy people, crazy people,
Old and young, bold and shy.

CHORUS
Lazy people, crazy people, etc.

(*Micaela enters.*)

MORALES
Now, there's a pretty girl approaching;
She seems to be shy and afraid.
Perhaps, but no!
She's too bashful, she needs coaching.

CHORUS
You do it then; go to her aid!

MORALES (*to Micaela*)
Young lady, may I help you?

MICAELA (*with simplicity*)
Yes, I'd like to speak to a guard.

MORALES (*with gallantry*)
You're in luck, I'm here!

MICAELA
No, I am looking for a soldier named
Don José.
Do you know him, too?

MORALES
Don José? Oh yes, of course we do.

MICAELA (*animatedly*)
You do? Perhaps you can tell me
where to find him?

MORALES
The company he's serving with has
not arrived yet.

MICAELA (*with disappointment*)
I see. Then he's not here?

MORALES
No, I am sorry, but don't you worry.
For very soon he will be here,
My pretty dear.
It won't be long, the bugle will be
blowing.
His company will come and we'll be
going.

CHORUS AND MORALES
It won't be long, the bugle will be
blowing.
His company will come and we'll be
going.

MORALES (*very gallantly*)
But may I suggest at present,
Since you have to wait, my dear,
You will find it far more pleasant
Inside the guardhouse than out here.

MICAELA
In there?

CHORUS
Why not?

MICAELA
With you?

CHORUS
With us!

MICAELA (*slyly*)
I'd better not.
All the same, I thank you a lot!

MORALES
You may enter without fear.
We will show you all respect,
And in ev'ry way, my dear,
We're most polite and correct.

MICAELA
I don't doubt your word.
Nonetheless, I'd rather go and then
return.
It's better so.
(*gently mocking*) For very soon the
bugle will be blowing.
His company will come and you'll be
going.

CHORUS, MICAELA AND MORALES
It won't be long, the bugle will be
blowing.
His company will come and you'll be
going.

(*The soldiers surround Micaela. She
tries to evade them.*)

MORALES
Why don't you stay?

MICAELA
No, no, I can't!

CHORUS
Why don't you stay?

MICAELA
No, no, I can't, no, no! I cannot!

CHORUS
Why don't you stay, don't go away.
Stay a little while, don't go away!

MICAELA (*escaping*)
Now good-bye. Some other day!

MORALES (*resignedly*)
Farewell to beauty,
Back to our duty.
Let's resume where we stopped before,
And watch the passing crowd once
more.

CHORUS
Lazy people, crazy people, etc.

No. 3 Chorus of Street boys

(*A bugle call is played. A military
march is heard at a distance. The
soldiers form in line in front of the
guardhouse. The relief appears; first
a bugler and fifer, then a crowd of
street boys. Lieutenant Zuniga and
Corporal Don José follow, then the
dragoons. During the street-boys'
chorus, the relief forms in front of
the guard going off duty.*)

CHILDREN
We are soldiers marching proudly,
Here we come to change the guard.
Boys, blow your bugles loudly!
Ta ra tatata ratata.
See us march in perfect manner,
We are never out of step.
Follow the waving banner,
One two, one two, hep, hep!
Straight in line beside our neighbors,
Shoulders back and heads up high,
We raise our trusty sabers
And salute you going by.
We are soldiers marching proudly,
Here we come to change the guard.
Boys, blow the bugles loudly!
Ta ra tatata ratata.
Company halt! Stand at ease!
Tarata tarata tarata tatata, taratata!

MORALES
I have a message for you from a
young and charming girl
who asked to speak to you . . .
Light blue skirt and very long braids.

JOSÉ
I am sure that was Micaela!

(*Exeunt guard going off duty. The
boys march off behind the bugler
and fifer of the retiring guard, in
the same manner as they followed
those of the relief.*)

CHILDREN
We are soldiers marching proudly,
Leaving with the changing guard.
Boys, blow your bugles loudly!
Taratatata ratata.
See us march, etc. . . .

No. 3 bis Recitative

ZUNIGA

Don José, is it true that in that
factory, there,
Many pretty women are working?

JOSÉ

Indeed, sir, that is so; and ev'rybody
knows
That these cigarette girls are of
very easy virtue.

ZUNIGA

Are they also easy to look at?

JOSÉ

Sir, I don't know much about that,
For I am not concerned with women
of that nature.

ZUNIGA

What concerns you, my friend, I think
I know.
You're in love with one charming
girl. Micaela is her name.
"Light blue skirt and very long
braids."
Well, am I right about that?

JOSÉ

I admit you are right! I confess,
she's the girl I love.
And as for the factory girls, when you
hear the bell
They'll be here. Then you can judge
their looks quite well.

No. 4 Chorus of Cigarette girls

(*The factory bell rings. José sits down
busying himself with repairing the
chain of his saber and pays no attention to the young men and the
townspeople entering. The bell stops
ringing.*)

TOWNSPEOPLE
YOUNG MEN

Ev'ry day at noon
You will find us here
Waiting for the time
When the girls appear
Charming to the eye.
How we love to court them
Hoping that our fond wishes
may come true
As all lovers do.
(*The cigarette girls enter, smoking.*)
Here they are, the bright-eyed
coquettes,

Keen and audacious,
Idly smoking their cigarettes,
And so flirtatious!

CIGARETTE GIRLS

Smoke rings make their lazy way,
Softly curling.
Skyward they stray,
In a fragrant cloud unfurling.
Their perfume pervades the air,
Gently stealing,
Soothing our mind
To a mellow pleasant feeling.
Those tender words you lovers say
every day
Fade away!
Your promises, too, like the smoke
in the blue,
Fade away.
Smoke rings rise and float away
In the blue of the sky.
See them curling and rising
And vanish at last in the blue of the
sky.
See them rise,
To the skies!

WORKING MEN

But where's Carmen today?
Why is she missing?

(*Carmen enters.*)

There she is!
Look at her!

CHORUS

Where she is, there is always
excitement!

YOUNG MEN (*to Carmen*)

At last! We've been anxiously waiting
for you!
We men want at least an answer
from you.
O Carmen, why must you tease us
this way?
When will you give your love?
Won't you name the day?

CARMEN

(*after a swift glance at José*)
When I'll give you my love?
Who knows, it's hard to tell!
Perhaps not at all,
Perhaps very soon!
(*resolutely*) But one thing I'll say:
Not today.

No. 5. Habanera

CARMEN

Love is free as the wayward breeze,
It can be shy, it can be bold.
Love can fascinate, love can tease,
Its whims and moods are thousandfold.
All at one it arrives and lingers,
For just how long can't be foretold.
Then it deftly slips through your
fingers,
For love's a thing no force can hold.
That's love for you,
That's love for you!

CHORUS

Love is free as the wayward breeze, etc.

CARMEN

A heart in love is quickly burned,
It knows no law except its own desire.
If I should love you and you spurn me,
I'm warning you, you play with fire!

CHORUS

You play with fire!

CARMEN

If I'm in love with you,
Don't ever, ever try to spurn me.

CHORUS

You play with fire!

CARMEN

My friend, remember, if I love you,
you play with fire!

CHORUS

A heart in love is quickly burned, etc.

CARMEN

Wait for love and you wait forever,
Don't wait at all, it comes to you.
Try to grasp it, it's far too clever,
It flies away into the blue.
Love has so many forms and shapes,
Each day it wears a new disguise.
Think you've caught it and it escapes
To catch you later by surprise.
That's love for you,
That's love for you!

CHORUS

Love has so many forms and
shapes, etc.

CARMEN

A heart in love is quickly burned, etc.

No. 6 Scene

YOUNG MEN (*to Carmen*)

Say when! Carmen, do not torment
us this way!
We men want a word of promise
today!
Carmen, please, do not tease!
Say, at least, which one you will
choose!

(*spoken over music*)

CARMEN

Hey, soldier, what are you doing here?

JOSÉ

I'm repairing the chain that holds my
saber.

CARMEN

Repairing the chain that holds your
saber!
Really! Is that *all* you want to hold?

(*The young men surround Carmen;
she looks first at them, then at José;
hesitates; turns as if going to factory,
then retraces her steps and goes
straight to José, who is still occupied
with his saber chain.*)

Look! Here's something to hold on to!

(*Carmen takes a flower from her bodice
and throws it at José. She runs
away.*)

No. 6 bis Recitative

(*There is a burst of laughter. The factory bell begins to ring again.
Exeunt working men, young men,
etc. The soldiers enter the guardhouse. José is left alone; he picks
up the flower, which has fallen at
his feet.*)

JOSÉ

What outrageous, scandalous
behaviour! And the way she threw
that flower at me! It came like a
dart! but its fragrance is sweet and
the flower is lovely. And the woman
. . . if it is true there are witches,
she is one! There can be no doubt.

(*Micaela enters.*)

MICAELA

José!

JOSÉ (*joyously*)

What a surprise!

MICAELA

There you are!

JOSÉ

Micaela!

MICAELA

I bring a message from your mother!

No. 7 Duet

JOSÉ (agitated)

So you come from my mother?
Tell me, how is my mother?

MICAELA (with simplicity)

She sends me with a message that will
    make you happy,
And a letter . . .

JOSÉ (joyfully)

MICAELA

And then some money, too,
To help along until your pay is due.
(hesitating) And then. . . .

JOSÉ

Go on . . .

MICAELA

And then . . . How can I tell you . . .
And then I also have another message
Which is of greater worth,
And, for a loving son,
Means more than all the gold on earth.

JOSÉ

That other message from my mother,
    won't you say?

MICAELA

You shall have it, too.
I promised to obey.
I'll pass it on to you.
After church I was walking homeward
    with your mother,
When she embraced me like her own
    child:
"My dear," she said to me,
"Make a trip to Seville.
You don't have far to travel,
And once you reach the city,
You'll go and find your way to José,
    my dear son.
You'll go and find my son, my beloved
    José.
Then say I implore God Almighty
To watch over him night and day.
Say that I'll never cease to love him;
That I forgive him, hope and pray."
Then she kissed me and said sincerely
As she sent me upon my way,
"Give this fond kiss he'll value dearly
From my heart to my son, José."

JOSÉ (deeply moved)

A kiss from my mother!

MICAELA

Yes, a kiss for her son.
(with simplicity) I give it now to you
As I was asked to do.

(She kisses José.)

JOSÉ (with emotion)

My heart is all aglow
With loving thoughts of my mother.
I see her dear beloved face,
I see my village and home.
Through all the years dear to me,
Mem'ries of long ago.
As I recall, my heart is all aglow,
My hope is bright and strong,
My soul restored with courage.
My heart is all aglow
As I recall my home and my beloved
    mother.

MICAELA

His heart is all aglow, etc.

JOSÉ (absorbedly)

Who knows what turn of fate might
    have shattered my hopes?
Even from far my mother shields
    her son,
(raptly) And with the kiss she
    sent to me
Has turned away the danger
And has made me strong.

MICAELA (animatedly)

Turn of fate, did you say?
Some danger you don't know?
Is there anything wrong?

JOSÉ

No, no! Let's speak of you, dear
    Micaela.
When do you intend to go home?

MICAELA

Soon, this very evening.
Tomorrow, I'll be with your mother.

JOSÉ (animatedly)

I'm so glad! And please, tell her
    for me:
Tell her my thoughts are always
    near her,
And say I repent what I've done.
And say that I shall not fail her,
She'll be proud of her son!
Now I bid you good-bye
As I send you upon your way.
Give her this kiss she'll value dearly
From the heart of her son, José.

(José kisses Micaela.)

MICAELA (with simplicity)

I'll tell her all you say,
That I promise to do,
And I'll give her from you
This kiss, my dear José.
Your heart is all aglow. . . . etc.

No. 7 bis Recitative

JOSÉ

Let me see what she wrote, while you
    stay here with me.

MICAELA

Oh no, I'd rather go and later I will
    come back.

JOSÉ

But why should you go?

MICAELA

I'd prefer it. I'd rather you read it
    without me.
Good-bye, until later on.

JOSÉ

You won't be long?

MICAELA

Not long at all.

(Exit Micaela)

JOSÉ (after having read the letter)

I'll obey, dear mother.
You need not be afraid.
I'll obey with a happy heart.
I give my solemn word
To marry Micaela
In spite of you! You and your flowers!

No. 8 Chorus

(The girls are heard screaming
behind the scene.)

ZUNIGA

Say, what is going on in there?
A letter?

SOPRANOS (on stage)

Hurry up, hurry up.
Can't somebody hear?

MEZZOS (on stage)

Hurry up, hurry up!
Someone interfere!

SOPRANOS

Carmen began the fight!

MEZZOS

No, no, **she didn't** do it!

SOPRANOS

She did it!

MEZZOS

Not at all!

SOPRANOS

I tell you, Carmen did it!
She was the first to strike a blow!

MEZZOS (to Zuniga)

They're telling you a lie!

SOPRANOS (to Zuniga)

They're telling you a lie!
Of course, it is a lie!

BOTH

It is a lie, it is a shameful lie,
They are telling a lie!

MEZZOS
(drawing Zuniga to their side)

This is how it came to pass:
When Manuela kept talking
That she had enough of walking,
She would go and buy an ass.

SOPRANOS (also drawing Zuniga
to their side)

Carmen shouted through the room,
(Maybe she tried to be funny):
"You would only waste your money,
You'd look better on a broom!"

MEZZOS

Manuela shouted back:
"You cat, you are only jealous!
You don't even have to tell us,
We know all your gypsy pack!"

SOPRANOS

"You can't buy a pair of shoes,
Let alone donkeys to ride on,
So why put that air of pride on?
And watch out whom you attack!"

ALL

And in just one moment more,
Both of them rolled on the floor,
And then and there
We saw the pair
Pulling at each other's hair!

ZUNIGA (impatiently)

The devil with this female squalling!
(to Don José) Listen, José, you go and
    take two men.
Go inside and find out what's the
    cause of this brawling.

(José enters the factory, followed by two soldiers.)

SOPRANOS

Carmen began the fight!

MEZZOS

No, no, she didn't do it!

SOPRANOS

I tell you that she did!

MEZZOS

She did not!

SOPRANOS

She was the first one to strike a blow!

ZUNIGA

Enough!
Somebody take all these females away!

SOPRANOS

But, sir!

MEZZOS

But, sir!

ALL

Don't listen to their lies!
We swear it isn't true,
It isn't true, it isn't true,
It isn't true at all!

SOPRANOS

Carmen began the fight.
She was the first to attack.

MEZZOS

No, she was in the right!
She only tried to hit back!

SOPRANOS

Carmen is to blame!

MEZZOS

Absolutely not!

SOPRANOS

Yes, yes, yes, yes, yes, yes!

MEZZOS

No, no, no, no, no, no!

ALL

It was she who struck the first blow!

SOPRANOS

Carmen began the fight!

MEZZOS

No, no, that isn't right!

(The soldiers clear the square. Carmen appears at the factory door, led by José and followed by the two soldiers.)

No. 9 Song and Melodrama

JOSÉ

Sir, it is true, two girls started a quarrel.
Only insults at first, later it came to blows.
One of them has been wounded.

ZUNIGA

And by whom?

JOSÉ

This one here, sir.

ZUNIGA *(to Carmen)*

You heard the report. What have you got to say?

CARMEN

Trala lalalalalala!
You can burn me alive,
I won't tell you a thing.
Trala lalalalalala!
You may flog me or torture me,
It doesn't matter!

ZUNIGA

Do us a favor and kindly stop.
I told you to answer my question.
Speak up!

CARMEN

(staring impudently at Zuniga)

Tra lalalalalala.
I will never betray
What I keep in my heart!
Tra lalalalalala.
There's one man I adore,
And he knows that I love him.

ZUNIGA

Since you are disposed to rebel,
You may practice your arias inside of a cell.

CHORUS OF WOMEN

Off with her, off to jail!

(Carmen strikes a woman who happens to be near her.)

ZUNIGA *(to Carmen)*

Confound you!
You are a menace to all those around you!

CARMEN

(with the utmost impertinence)

Tra lalalalalalalalalalalala!

ZUNIGA

It's a shame, though,
She's such a wildcat!
For she has spirit and wit!
But we must tame her just a bit.
Tie her hands behind her back!

(He goes into the guardhouse.)

CARMEN

Where are you going to take me?

JOSÉ

You go to jail, and no one can prevent it.

CARMEN

Indeed, no one can prevent it?

JOSÉ

That's right. I must do as I'm told.

CARMEN

Even so, I will bet that no matter how strict the order,
You will help me to escape. You know why? Because you love me.

JOSÉ

I, love you?

CARMEN

Yes, José! The flower I gave you today, the flower you hid there in your jacket,
You might as well throw it away, it has done its duty.

JOSÉ

You're going too far! Once and for all, you must not talk. That's a command!

CARMEN

(speaks, while music goes on)

Very well, General, very well!
You forbid me to talk, so I won't talk.

No. 10 Seguidilla and Duet

CARMEN

Close to the wall of Sevilla,
I know a certain old tavern.
I go there to dance seguidilla
And to drink Manzanilla,
At the inn of Señor Lillas Pastia.
But when a girl goes out to dance,
She wants to have some company.
So I don't want to take a chance,
I'll take the man I love with me.
(laughing) The man I love?
What am I saying?
I told him yesterday we're through.

My heart is free, longing for someone,
Eager for love with someone new.
There are so many who adore me
But I don't care for any one.
With one whole Sunday free before me,
Who wants my love? He'll be the one.
Who wants my heart?
Who comes to claim it?
Here is your chance, it still is free.
You can have it for the asking.
With my new love I'm on my way.
Close to the wall of Sevilla,
I know a certain old tavern.
I go there to dance seguidilla
And drink Manzanilla.
I will meet my love at Lillas Pastia's inn!

JOSÉ *(with severity)*

Enough! For the last time, I forbid you to talk!

CARMEN *(with simplicity)*

I do not talk to you. I sing for my own pleasure,
And I'm thinking!
And ev'rybody knows thoughts are free.
I'm thinking of one certain man,
An officer who might be you,
Who loves me, and, I am sure,
Yes, I confess that I could love him, too.

JOSÉ

Carmen!

CARMEN *(pointedly)*

This certain soldier is not of high standing;
Really, his rank is quite low.
To tell you the truth, he's a corp'ral.
But why should I be demanding?
I'll be happy with him, I know.

JOSÉ *(agitated)*

Carmen, I can bear it no longer!
If I free you, if I surrender,
Will you promise to keep your word?
And if I love you, Carmen,
Will you return my love?

CARMEN

Yes.

JOSÉ

At Lillas Pastia's —

CARMEN

We both will dance the seguidilla,

JOSÉ

I have your word?

CARMEN

And we will drink Manzanilla.

JOSÉ

(*He unties the rope.*)

You'll keep your word!

CARMEN

Ah!
Close to the wall of Sevilla,
I know a certain old tavern.
Together we'll dance seguidilla
And we'll drink Manzanilla!
Tra lalalalalalala!

No. 11 Finale

(*Zuniga comes out of the guardhouse.*)

ZUNIGA (*to José*)

Here's the order, José.
Now go and do your duty.

CARMEN (*aside to José*)

You pretend to lead me away.
Stay in back of me
(*making a backward gesture with her head*)
And I'll give you a heavy push.
Turn around, as you fall,
The rest I will take care of.
(*in a different tone; singing and laughing in Zuniga's face*)
A heart in love is quickly burned,
It knows no law except its own desire.
If I should love you and you spurn me,
I'm warning you, you play with fire!
If I'm in love with you,
Don't ever, ever try to spurn me!
My friend, remember, if I love you,
You play with fire!

(*She marches off with José. At the bridge Carmen pushes him. He falls down and she escapes, laughing loudly.*)

ACT II

(*Lillas Pastia's Inn. When the curtain rises, Carmen, Frasquita and Mercedes are discovered seated at a table with the officers. The gypsy girls dance, accompanied by gypsies playing the guitar and tambourine. At the end of the dance the song begins.*)

No. 12 Gypsy Song

CARMEN

The stillness at the end of day
Is broken by a lazy jingle,

The sleepy air begins to tingle.
The gypsy dance is under way!
And soon the tambourines of Spain
And strumming of guitars competing,
Continue on and on, repeating
The same old song, the same old strain,
The same old song, the same refrain.
Tra lalalalalala!

FRASQUITA AND MERCEDES

(*The dance continues.*)

Tra lalalalalalala.

(*The dance ceases.*)

CARMEN

The copper rings the gypsies wear
Against their dusky skins are gleaming,
With red and orange colors streaming,
Swirling skirts billow through the air!
The music guides the dancing feet
With ever more compelling beat.
Quite timid first, but soon the master,
It drives them on, and growing faster,
It starts to rise and rise to fever heat!
Tra lalalalalala!

FRASQUITA AND MERCEDES

(*The dance continues.*)

Tra lalalalalalala!

(*The dance ceases.*)

CARMEN

The gypsy men play on with fire!
Their tambourines loudly whirring!
The pulsing rhythm fiercely stirring,
Enflames the gypsy girls' desire.
Their passion carries them away,
Their agile bodies turn and sway
In burning frenzy and abandon.
On and on they dance, madly driven,
Like a whirlwind no force can stay!
Tra lalalalalala!

FRASQUITA AND MERCEDES

(*The dance continues.*)

Tra lalalalalalala!

(*Carmen, Frasquita and Mercedes join the dance.*)

No. 12 bis Recitative

FRASQUITA

My friends, Pastia just said . . .

ZUNIGA

What is that he said, Lillas Pastia?

FRASQUITA

He said that the chief-of-police told him the inn should be closing.

ZUNIGA

All right, then, let us go. You girls will come with us.

FRASQUITA

We can't. We have to stay.

ZUNIGA

But Carmen, you? You'll come with us? You're silent.
I think I know why: you are cross.

CARMEN

I should be cross! But why?

ZUNIGA

On account of the boy who went to jail for you.

CARMEN

What has happened to the poor lad?

ZUNIGA

They released him today.

CARMEN

They released him? I'm glad!
And now, to all of you, good night!

ALL THREE GIRLS

And now to all of you, good night!

No. 13 Chorus

CHORUS OF MEN (*off stage*)

Hurrah, hurrah, the Toréro!
Hurrah, hurrah, Escamillo!

ZUNIGA

They're having a torchlight parade!
They're going wild cheering Escamillo!
(*toward the street*)
We all would be proud, Toréro, if you would join us.
We'll toast your former triumphs, and all the ones to come!

(*Escamillo enters.*)

CHORUS AND SOLOISTS (*on stage*)

Hurrah, hurrah, the Toréro!
Hurrah, hurrah, Escamillo!
Hurrah!

No. 14 Toreador Song

ESCAMILLO

Thank you all, you gallant soldier-heroes,

And in return I drink to you tonight!
Long may you soldiers and we Toréros
Live to share a common joy,
The thrill of the fight!
Crowds are swarming in the great arena,
Excitement fills the atmosphere.
Ev'ryone waiting, loudly debating,
Wild with impatience,
They raise a thunderous cheer!
Shouts and stamping become contagious,
Till at last it's like a thunderstorm.
Day of fame for men of soul courageous,
Day of fame for men of heart!
It's time, Toréro, come on! On guard! Ah!
Toreador, fight well and hard,
Proud as a king,
Yours is the ring!
And, after you have won the victor's crown,
Earn your sweet reward,
Your señorita's love!
Toreador, your sweet reward is love!

ALL

Toreador, fight well and hard, etc. . . . .

ESCAMILLO

All at once, the crowd is silent.
What are they waiting for?
And what is happening?
Breathless expectancy
Hushes the gallery.
Through the gate the bull is leaping out into the ring!
Rushing on, he charges madly,
A horse goes under, dragging down a picador.
"Come on, Toréro!"
They roar like thunder.
Then, like a flash, the bull turns 'round,
Charging once more!
The lances stab his bleeding shoulder,
And blind with rage he runs.
The sand is red with blood!
Clear the ring, ev'ryone take cover!
Just one man stands sword in hand!
It's time, Toréro, come on! On guard! Ah!
Toreador, etc. . . . .

ALL

Toreador, etc. . . .

MERCEDES

Your love!

ESCAMILLO

Your love!

FRASQUITA

Your love!

CARMEN (*looking at Escamillo*)

Your love!

ESCAMILLO (*looking at Carmen*)

Your love!

ALL

Toreador, Toreador!
Your prize is love!

No. 14A Recitative

ESCAMILLO

Señorita, one word. I'd like to know
  your name. And when I fight again,
  it shall be on my lips.

CARMEN

My name? It's Carmen. Or else,
  Carmencita.

ESCAMILLO

And if I would say that I love you?

CARMEN

Then I would say you are wasting your
  time.

ESCAMILLO

That does not sound very inviting.
  And I've no other choice but to
  hope and keep waiting.

CARMEN

I can't stop you from waiting, and to
  hope is always sweet.

ZUNIGA

Since you have decided to stay, I shall
  come back.

CARMEN

That would be a mistake!

ZUNIGA

Bah! That risk I will take!

ESCAMILLO (*spoken*)

My friends, I thank you all!

(*He leaves.*)

No. 14B

Exit of Escamillo

No. 14C Recitative

FRASQUITA

Tell us quickly, what are you
  planning?

EL DANCAIRO

We're handling goods coming from
England. I'm sure we'll get them
through in the usual way. But you
three girls must go along.

FRASQUITA, MERCEDES, CARMEN

We'll go along?

EL DANCAIRO

I must be sure nothing goes wrong.

No. 15 Quintet

EL DANCAIRO

This is a superb proposition.

MERCEDES

Another deal in contraband?

FRASQUITA

Another deal in contraband?

EL DANCAIRO

We will earn a nice fat commission,
But we need you to lend a hand.

EL REMENDADO

Yes, we need you to lend a hand.

CARMEN

You do?

EL DANCAIRO

We do!

FRASQUITA

You do?

EL REMENDADO

We do!

ALL

So you (yes, we) need us (you) to
  lend a hand.

EL REMENDADO AND EL DANCAIRO

We might as well admit as much,
This bus'ness needs a woman's touch.
When it's a case of double dealing,
Lying or stealing,
Better concealing,
It happens time and time again,
Women are more subtle than men.
In addition,
Their intuition
Can turn a guess to sure success!

FRASQUITA, MERCEDES, CARMEN

Yes, you might as well confess,
We turn a guess to sure success.

EL REMENDADO AND EL DANCAIRO

Now don't you girls agree with me?

FRASQUITA, MERCEDES, CARMEN

Of course, why should we disagree?

EL REMENDADO AND EL DANCAIRO

I'm glad that you agree with me.

ALL

Yes, in any case etc. . . . .

EL DANCAIRO

All right, agreed. We'll go today.

FRASQUITA

Just as you say.

MERCEDES

Just as you say.

EL DANCAIRO

Then let us hurry.

CARMEN

Wait, not so fast. I say no.
If you all want to go, then go!
But this time our plans seem to vary.
I'm staying here.

EL REMENDADO AND EL DANCAIRO

Please say you'll join us, Carmen dear.

CARMEN

Say what you will, I'm staying here.

EL REMENDADO AND EL DANCAIRO

You do not want to be contrary.
The plans are made, why interfere?

CARMEN

You heard it all, I'm staying here.

FRASQUITA AND MERCEDES

Say you will come, Carmen dear.

EL DANCAIRO

But, at least, tell us why.

THE OTHERS

Tell us why!

CARMEN

I'll tell you what you want to know.

THE OTHERS

Go on!

CARMEN

The reason I refuse to go . . .

EL REMENDADO AND EL DANCAIRO

Is what?

FRASQUITA AND MERCEDES

Is what?

CARMEN

That I am in love again!

EL REMENDADO AND EL DANCAIRO

Did I hear right?

FRASQUITA AND MERCEDES

She merely said she is in love.

ALL (*except Carmen*)

She's in love!

EL DANCAIRO

Come on, my dear, say you don't
  mean it!

CARMEN

I'm in love as never before!

EL REMENDADO AND EL DANCAIRO

We must admit we are astounded,
Because you've shown us more
  than once
How easy you have always found it
To combine your duty with love.
You know well, very well,
How to combine your duty with love!

CARMEN

You know that I would join
  you gladly
In this new plan you've spoken of!
Though I may disappoint you badly,
Just this once, love comes first.
This evening duty must yield to love!

EL DANCAIRO

You mean you will not change
  your mind?

CARMEN

No, I will not.

EL REMENDADO

But look, you simply cannot leave us so!

ALL

Say you will go, be nice, say you
  will go!

EL REMENDADO AND EL DANCAIRO

We need you there —

FRASQUITA AND MERCEDES

To do your share.

EL REMENDADO AND EL DANCAIRO

You know it's true!

FRASQUITA AND MERCEDES

You know it's true!

CARMEN
In that respect, I will agree with you.

ALL
When it's a case of double dealing,
etc. . . .

No. 15 bis Recitative

EL DANCAIRO
Who is the lucky man?

CARMEN
If you must know, it's a soldier of the guard, who, in order to help me, went to prison for me.

EL REMENDADO
A most beautiful thought!

EL DANCAIRO
It may be that your man has become less obliging.
How do you know that he will come?

No. 16 SONG

(behind the scene, far away)

JOSÉ
"Who are you?
Someone new?
Soldier, who goes there?"

CARMEN
Do you hear?
I was right!

JOSÉ *(as before)*
Where are you going to?
Soldier, tell me where?"
"Looking for my rival,
I intend to meet him,
Fight him and defeat him."
"Since the case is so
Freely you may go.
Honor's stern command,
Affairs of the heart,
Those are things apart.
Soldiers understand."

FRASQUITA
That's a handsome boy!

MERCEDES
A very handsome boy!

EL DANCAIRO
Men like that we need to have on our side!

EL REMENDADO
Tell him to join us!

CARMEN
That he'll never do.

EL REMENDADO
It is worth a try.

CARMEN
Good, at least I'll try.
(The voice approaches little by little.)

JOSÉ
"Who are you?
Someone new?
Soldier, who goes there?
Where are you going to?
Soldier, tell me where?"
"Faithful to my sweetheart,
Mine's a lover's mission
In the old tradition, etc."

No. 16 bis Recitative

CARMEN
You're here at last!

JOSÉ
Carmen!

CARMEN
You had to go to jail?

JOSÉ
For all of two months.

CARMEN
You complain?

JOSÉ
Not a bit!
And, if it were for your sake, they could have kept me longer.

CARMEN
Then you love me?

JOSÉ
Love you? I adore you!

CARMEN
We have been visited by your superiors. They had us sing and dance.

JOSÉ
Not you, too?

CARMEN *(ironically)*
Bless my soul, I'll bet that you are jealous!

JOSÉ
Of course! And why not?

CARMEN
Calm down, my friend, calm down.

No. 17 DUET

CARMEN *(gaily)*
Now that you're here, I'll dance for you,
For you alone, señor.
And even more than that, I'll sing and play my music.
(She makes José sit down.)
You sit right here, Don José.
(with a serio-comic air) You're the audience!
(She dances accompanying herself with the castanets. Near the end of the dance bugles are heard behind the scenes.)

JOSÉ *(stopping Carmen)*
Just one moment, wait,
Only one moment, I beg you!

CARMEN *(surprised)*
And just why, may I ask?

JOSÉ
In the distance I hear . . .
Yes, our bugles are blowing,
Sounding the retreat.
Now, don't you hear them, too?

CARMEN *(gaily)*
Bravo, bravo! That's even better!
It's not an easy thing to sing and dance without music,
But now we have some music which has dropped from the sky.
(She resumes her dancing. The sound of the bugles dies away.)
Lalalalalalala.

JOSÉ *(again stopping Carmen)*
You do not understand, my love!
That was the signal,
I must be back, in camp,
In my quarters by night.

CARMEN
(stupified) Back in camp? For the night?
(with an outburst) Ah, how could I be so stupid!
I took no end of pains,
I tried my very best,
My very, very best
To entertain my guest!
So I sang and I danced,
Thinking **(may God forgive me)**
I was almost in love!

Taratata!
He hears the blasted bugle!
Taratata!
Dear me, and off he goes!
Back to camp, stupid fool!
Here! *(throwing his shako at him)*
Take your belt, your saber and your helmet,
And go back to your camp, my boy!
Hurry back to your quarters!

JOSÉ *(sadly)*
You're very wrong, you know,
To mock me as you do!
I do not want to go!
You must believe me, Carmen,
And I confess to you,
No one before has thrilled my heart like you,
No woman on this earth
Has stirred my heart so deeply!

CARMEN
Taratata! "My God, retreat is sounding!"
Taratata! "I'm going to be late!"
Oh my God, there are the bugles,
I'm afraid I'll be late!"
So he forgets me, runs off.
That's the end of his love!

JOSÉ
And so, you don't believe my love is real!

CARMEN
I don't!

JOSÉ
Well then, you do not know!

CARMEN
What more is there to know?

JOSÉ
Listen to me!

CARMEN
You'll keep them waiting!

JOSÉ *(violently)*
Yes, I say you will!

CARMEN
No, no, no, no!

JOSÉ
I want it so!
(He draws, from the vest of his uniform, the flower which Carmen threw at him and shows it to her.)
Through ev'ry **long and lonely** hour

In prison there, I kept your flower,
And though its bloom was swiftly gone,
Its haunting fragrance lingered on.
In the darkness, as I lay dreaming,
Its perfume consoling, redeeming,
Recalled your image night and day,
And my despair would fade away.
Another time, I would berate you,
I swore to detest and to hate you!
Of what nemesis am I the prey?
What whim of fate sent you my way?
Then I realized I was lying;
There could be no doubt, no denying,
One burning hope was all I knew,
One sole desire inflamed my heart!
Carmen, I longed for you,
  I longed for you!
Carmen, the magic of your glances
Cast a spell around my heart.
Luring me on like an enchantress,
You ruled my soul! You took
  possession of my heart!
Carmen, I love you!

CARMEN

No, I don't call that love!

JOSÉ

What did you say?

CARMEN

No, you do not love me,
No, no, for if you did, you see,
You'd come with me!

JOSÉ

Carmen!

CARMEN

People in love belong together,
They cannot bear to be apart.
Carry me off and far away,
Over the highest hills and deepest
  valleys.
I would know that you love me then!
Carry me far across the mountains,

JOSÉ (disconcerted)

Carmen!

CARMEN

Sharing adventures day by day.
Take me away and prove your love!
At liberty coming and going,
No silly rules or officers there to obey.
No stupid retreat ever blowing,
Bidding the lovers part at the end of
  the day.
Happy to roam the open spaces,
All the world for our home,
We obey our will alone!
Best of all, a priceless possession,
Our life is free!

JOSÉ

My God!

CARMEN

People in love, etc. . . . .

JOSÉ
(in painful resolution) Carmen, please,
No more! I beg of you, no more!
No, Carmen, no, no more!
O have pity, Carmen!
  (wresting himself away from
    Carmen's embraces)
No, I cannot do what you say!
Deserting my flag and betray . . .
That's dishonor, that's degradation.
That I won't do!

CARMEN (harshly)

Well, then, go!

JOSÉ (imploringly)

Carmen, please have mercy!

CARMEN

No, I'm finished with you!

JOSÉ

I beg you!

CARMEN

How I hate you! Good-bye!
It's good-bye once for all!

JOSÉ (grievingly)

So then once for all, good-bye!

CARMEN

At last!

JOSÉ

Farewell! Good-bye, once for all!

CARMEN

Good-bye!
(José goes toward the door; as he is
  about to open it, someone knocks.
  Silence)

No. 18 FINALE

ZUNIGA (from outside)
Hello, Carmen, hello, hello!

JOSÉ

Who is it? Who is there?

CARMEN

Be still, be still!

ZUNIGA
(enters after forcing the door)
What's going on there, I ask you!
  (He sees José)
(to Carmen) Oh, shame, my lovely
  Carmen,

Your taste is rather poor!
When there's an officer
Who offers so much more,
It's a private you prefer!
(to José) Get out, and hurry!

JOSÉ (calmly but resolutely)

No!

ZUNIGA (sternly)

Get out, there is the door!

JOSÉ (firmly)

I don't intend to go!

ZUNIGA (menacing José)

Scoundrel!

JOSÉ
(seizing his saber)
Damnation! I'll show you who will go!

CARMEN
(throwing herself between them)
You're mad, you jealous fool!
  (calls toward the adjoining room)
Come here, come here!
(The gypsies appear from every side.
At a sign from Carmen, El Dancairo
and El Remendado seize Zuniga and
      disarm him.)

CARMEN (to Zuniga, in a
      mocking tone)
It is a shame,
My gallant captain!
Love has played a nasty trick on you!
Your call was badly timed.
Too bad! And so we must resort,
For we cannot risk being caught,
To keep you here with us for our
  protection!.

EL REMENDADO AND EL DANCAIRO
(to Zuniga, pistols in hand, with the
      utmost politeness)
It breaks my heart,
But you and I are going in the same
  direction.
You'll come along with us?

CARMEN (laughing)

Consider the diversion!

EL REMENDADO AND EL DANCAIRO

What do you say?

CHORUS OF MEN

We'll go on this excursion.

ZUNIGA
(accepting the situation with
    good grace)
Why, yes, of course, I accept!
For as matters stand,
Your invitation is a most convincing
  one!
(in a merry tone) But, later on,
  watch out!

EL DANCAIRO (philosophically)
I'm sorry, such is life, sir!
Let's think of that some other day!
You have the honor of leading
  the way!

EL REMENDADO AND MEN
You have the honor of leading
  the way!

CARMEN (to José)
Have you at last made up your mind?

JOSÉ (sighing)
I have no choice!

CARMEN

Ah, that does not sound too kind,
But, no matter! For soon you will see
What life can be!
Happy to roam the open spaces,
All the world for our home,
We obey our will alone.
Best of all, a priceless possession,
Our life is free!

CHORUS OF WOMEN (to José)
Come follow us into the mountains,
Be one of us, be our companion.
Come with us and you will see
What life can be,
Once you are really free!

CHORUS OF MEN (to José)
Be one of us, and you will see
What life can be,
Once you are free!

ALL

Happy to roam the open spaces,
All the world for a home,
We obey our will alone.
Best of all, a priceless possession,
Our life is free!

ACT III

(A wild spot in the mountains. As the
curtain rises a few of the smugglers are
seen lying about, enveloped in their
cloaks. The gypsies enter.)

No. 19 SEXTET and CHORUS

SMUGGLERS

Be cautious, be cautious,
Ev'ryone remember,
There before us gold and riches loom;
But remember, the path is
    dang'rous,
A faulty step may be your doom!

FRASQUITA, MERCEDES, CARMEN, JOSÉ,
EL REMENDADO AND EL DANCAIRO

This is the life, the life we want
    to lead,
But he who leads it must possess
The courage of the fearless!
We must be keen, alert and unafraid,
For danger lies at ev'ry turn,
At ev'ry hour it's near us!
On our way, unconcerned,
Come what may, we prevail
Through the hazardous storm,
While the thunder is rolling!
Toward our goal, undeterred,
We proceed without fail,
Never minding the vigilant soldier
    patrolling!
We will get to our goal, come
    what may!

ALL

Be cautious, be cautious, etc.

No. 19 bis Recitative

EL DANCAIRO

You all may take a little rest, while
    you can get it. Meanwhile I want to
    make quite sure that there'll be no
    surprises. We can't take any chances,
    our merchandise must get through!

CARMEN (*to José*)

Why do you stare like that?

JOSÉ

I was thinking that there in the valley
    lives a kind and God-fearing woman
    who believes me to be honest. I have
    not kept her faith!

CARMEN

And who is that sweet lady?

JOSÉ

I am warning you, Carmen, watch
    what you say; she is my mother!

CARMEN

I see. Then you should go home to your
    mother. The kind of life we lead is
    not for you. And you might as well
    leave us, the sooner the better.

JOSÉ

You say that I should leave?

CARMEN

Precisely!

JOSÉ

And go away from you? I warn you,
    if you say that once more . . .

CARMEN

You mean that you would kill me?
How fierce you look!
You don't say a word. It is all in the
    cards, we have no way to change it!

No. 20 Trio

(*Frasquita and Mercedes spread cards
before them.*)

FRASQUITA AND MERCEDES

Shuffle, shuffle!
Now then, now then!
Come, let us try!

MERCEDES

Three cards to the right,

FRASQUITA

Three cards to the left.

MERCEDES

Four above.

FRASQUITA

Four below.

FRASQUITA AND MERCEDES

The cards will say what joy or sorrow
They hold in store, what luck
    we'll have tomorrow,
Which lover will be treacherous,
And which one will be true to us.
We want to know
Which one we should be wary of,
Which man will be our own true love.
Let's see! Let's see!

FRASQUITA

See, my man is youthful and bold,
One lover with daring and courage.

MERCEDES

And my suitor is very old,
But he's rich and offers me marriage.

FRASQUITA (*haughtily*)

Then he lifts me up on his horse
And speeds me away to the mountains!

MERCEDES

We live in a palace, of course,
With gardens and statues and
    fountains.

FRASQUITA

And his ardor never grows cold,
Every day unending embraces.

MERCEDES

I've barrels and barrels of gold,
Diamonds, pearls, satins and laces!

FRASQUITA

My goodness, this is a surprise!
My man is a powerful pirate.

MERCEDES (*joyfully*)

And mine, and mine . . . can I credit
    my eyes?
He . . . he dies! Ah, I'm his widow
    and heiress.

BOTH

Let's try again, we may discover
Important traits about our future lover.
Which suitor will be treacherous, etc. . .

MERCEDES

An heiress!

FRASQUITA

A lover!

CARMEN

Let's see what the cards hold for me.
(*She turns up the cards, on her side.*)
Diamonds! Spades!
It's death! It is plain.
First for me, then for him,
But all the same, it's death!
You can't evade the truth the cards
    are saying clearly,
No matter how you try.
No use to deal again, they're telling
    you sincerely,
The cards will never lie!
If Fate saved you a happy page
    within its book,
No need for anxiousness.
You know you'll get a lucky card
    before you look,
Your fate is happiness.
But if your time has come and you
    are evil-starred,
And if the end is near,
You can try twenty times, the
    unrelenting card
Will reappear once more; if you are
    evil-starred,
If there is death in store
The unrelenting card will reappear
    once more!

(*turning up the cards*)
Once more, once more,
There's death in store.

FRASQUITA AND MERCEDES
(*joining Carmen*)

We want to know etc. . . .

CARMEN (*continuing*)

Once more! For me it's death, etc . . .

No. 20 bis Recitative

CARMEN

What news?

EL DANCAIRO

Quite good! We might as well move
    on, we have an even chance.
And you, José, stay here.
You will shoot on sight if need be.

FRASQUITA

You think we'll have clear sailing?

EL DANCAIRO

Yes, except for one spot. Close to the
    pass, three guards are on patrol.
That might mean trouble.
We must get them out of the way.

CARMEN

This is an assignment for us.
We must get through and so we shall!

No. 21 Ensemble with Chorus

WOMEN, CARMEN,
FRASQUITA AND MERCEDES

All men are weak and fond of women,
So are the guards, they're only human.
They're eager and anxious to be nice,
So we'll go ahead and break the ice.

THE THREE WOMEN AND FULL CHORUS

All men are weak, etc. . . . .

ALL

It won't be hard!

CARMEN

We will catch the guards off guard!

ALL

They will be nice.

FRASQUITA

To us women, more than nice!

MERCEDES

Yes, to us women they will be more
    than nice!

THE THREE WOMEN AND CHORUS
All men are weak and fond of women,
So are the guards, they're only human.
They're eager and anxious to be nice.
We must succeed at any price!

FRASQUITA, MERCEDES, CARMEN
It won't be hard, there's nothing to it,
Just keep the guards happy awhile.
They like to flirt, we let them do it.
No one gets hurt giving a smile.
And if we add one or two kisses
For our success, it's worth a try!

CHORUS OF WOMEN (jointly)
Here's the answer, it never misses,
Our contraband always gets by!

FRASQUITA, MERCEDES, CARMEN
Go ahead, come on, let's go!
Clear the way!

ALL
All men are weak, etc. . . . .
Clear the way, clear the way!

FRASQUITA, MERCEDES, CARMEN
We will clear the way for you all!

THE OTHERS
They will clear the way for us all!
(They all leave.)

No. 22 Aria
MICAELA
Here's where the smugglers hide
With their contraband booty;
So it is here I'll find José,
And for his mother's sake I'll do
  my duty,
For her sake conquer ev'ry fear.
I thought I could master my terror.
I was so sure I would be brave
  and strong.
But now, too late, I see my error!
Deep in my heart I know I was wrong!
Here in this dread surrounding
I'm alone and afraid,
But I will not despair!
God in His kindness all-abounding
Will make me strong and hear
  my prayer.
I'll be face to face with that woman
Who, with the blackest arts of hell,
Made a lawless man and a traitor
Of him I used to love so well.
She's dangerous, too, and alluring,
But she can't hurt me any more!
No, no, she can't hurt me any more!
I will speak to José right before her!
Ah! I place my hope and faith in
  Thee,

O Lord, dear God, watch over me!
Ah!
Make me strong and protect me!
Watch over me, God above!
Watch over me,
My Lord!

No. 22 bis Recitative
MICAELA
High up there on the rocks, it's he!
That's José. José, come here, José!
He has not heard me yet!
He has a gun! He is aiming!
Don José! (José fires a shot.)
Dear God, what shall I do?
I don't know where to turn.
(She disappears behind the rocks.)

ESCAMILLO (entering)
Just one inch further down
And all would have been over.

JOSÉ
Who are you? What's your name?

ESCAMILLO
Hey, easy now, my boy!

No. 23 Duo
ESCAMILLO
My name is Escamillo,
Toreador of Granada.

JOSÉ
Escamillo!

ESCAMILLO
That's right.

JOSÉ
Then I welcome you here.
You have a famous name.
But really, you were foolish to take
  so great a risk!

ESCAMILLO (carelessly)
Yes, there you may be right.
But you see, I'm in love, my friend,
And love takes chances;
(gaily) And any man, indeed, would
  not be worth his salt,
Who would not risk his life pursuing
  his romances.

JOSÉ
Then the one you love must be here?

ESCAMILLO
Right you are.
A most exciting gypsy girl!

JOSÉ
What is her name?

ESCAMILLO
Carmen.

JOSÉ (aside)
Carmen?

ESCAMILLO
It is. That's her name.
The way the rumor goes
She loved another man,
A soldier who deserted his brigade
  to please her.

JOSÉ (aside)
Carmen!

ESCAMILLO
A mad affair, but that of course was
  once,
For the loves of a Carmen do not
  last six months.

JOSÉ
You don't mind that at all?

ESCAMILLO
I love her, yes, I do.
I love her, my friend,
I love her madly!

JOSÉ
But when anyone takes a gypsy from
  her people,
You know, of course, he has to pay?

ESCAMILLO (gaily)
Good, then I'll pay, yes, I will pay.

JOSÉ (threateningly)
The price is to be paid with knives
  to the finish!

ESCAMILLO (surprised)
With knives to the finish?

JOSÉ
You understand?

ESCAMILLO (ironically)
Why, of course, now I do!
That fine dragoon deserter she's in
  love with,
Or rather was in love with, . . .
That is you!

JOSÉ (menacingly)
Yes, I'm the one!

ESCAMILLO
Oh, what a treat, my boy,
I'm overcome with joy.
Now I know where I stand.

BOTH
What stroke of good fortune
To find my rival here.

JOSÉ
His blood will flow before
  his sweetheart.
This will cost him dear.

ESCAMILLO
I look for his sweetheart
And find her cavalier.

BOTH
Man to man, I dare you,
Defend your life!

JOSÉ
We'll fight to the end
At the point of the knife!

ESCAMILLO
I welcome the challenge
To draw my knife!

BOTH
One of us must fall,
Defend your life!
Now draw your knife. On guard.
Defend your life!
(They fight. Escamillo slips and falls.
José is about to strike him when
Carmen enters.)

No. 24 Finale
CARMEN
(arresting José's arm)
Hold on, hold on, José!

ESCAMILLO (to Carmen)
Ah, the thought is enchanting!
I am a lucky man to owe my life to
  Carmen!
(to José, jauntily but haughtily)
As for you, soldier friend,
The fight is undecided,
But we'll renew the duel.
Whatever day you choose,
I'll be at your command.

EL DANCAIRO
(interposing)
No more of that, and no more quarrels.
Come, we're anxious to leave!
Let's go, and you go, too, my friend!

ESCAMILLO
Just one thing more, and then I shall
  be on my way:
May I invite you all
To the bullfight in Seville.
I'll do my very best to do honor to you.
All my friends will be there,
  (with a look at Carmen)
All my friends will be there.
(cooly to José, who makes a menacing
  gesture)
And you, not so ferocious!
  (gazing at Carmen)

Time will tell, yes, time will tell.
So till we meet again,
I bid you all farewell!
(*Escamillo exits slowly. José tries to attack him but is held back by El Dancairo and El Remendado.*)

JOSÉ
(*to Carmen, menacingly but restrainedly*)
This is enough, you hear!
Do not drive me too far!

EL DANCAIRO
Get ready, companions, it's time to start.

CHORUS
Get ready, get ready, companions, it's time to start!

EL REMENDADO
Stop! Someone is hiding there behind the rocks!
(*He brings Micaela forward.*)

CARMEN
It's a woman!

EL DANCAIRO
What luck! We have caught her in time!

JOSÉ (*recognizing Micaela*)
You! Micaela!

MICAELA (*joyously*)
Don José!

JOSÉ
Micaela! What folly brings you here?

MICAELA
I, I came here to find you!
I came here to remind you
Of someone dear to you.
A lonely mother is waiting sadly,
Longing for her son.
She is grieving for you and needs you.
She is kind and she will forgive.
Go to her, I implore you.
José, ah, José,
Come home with me,
Come home with me!

CARMEN (*to José*)
Go on, go on, it's better thus,
You never did belong to us!

JOSÉ (*to Carmen*)
So you want me to leave you?

CARMEN
Yes, you had better go.

JOSÉ
So you want me to leave you
So that you can quickly run off,
Into Escamillo's arms!
No, that you won't!
(*resolutely*) I swear, I won't leave you ever.
I won't go, I swear I never will,
You and I belong together,
Till the end for good or ill!
I swear I won't leave you ever,
I won't leave until the day I die.

ALL (*to José*)
This may cost you very dearly,
José, you're tempting your fate.
If you stay, it will be folly.
You must go before it's too late.

MICAELA (*to José*)
Hear what I say, I implore,
José, do not tempt your fate.
If you stay, it will be folly;
José, it is not too late.

JOSÉ (*to Micaela*)
Let me go!

MICAELA
You must give in!

JOSÉ
There is no turning back!
(*He seizes Carmen in a transport of passion.*)

ALL
José, we warn you!

JOSÉ
You are mine, and mine you stay.
You are mine, and I'll never let you go!
I will force you to obey,
Our destiny willed it so!
I swear, I won't let you leave me,
No, I won't until my dying day!

ALL
Stop! Go easy, we warn you, Don José!

MICAELA
(*authoritatively*) Just one more word I'll say,
And then I shall leave!
(*sadly*) You see, José, your mother is ill,
She is dying. You must not let her **die** without blessing her son!

JOSÉ
My mother, she is dying!

MICAELA
Yes, Don José!

JOSÉ
Then come, let us go!
(*He takes a few steps, then stops and speaks to Carmen.*)
Have you way then, I'll go.
But, we shall meet again!
(*José leads Micaela away; hearing Escamillo's voice he pauses, hesitating.*)

ESCAMILLO (*behind the scenes*)
Toreador, fight well and hard,
Proud as a king,
Yours is the ring.
(*Carmen rushes toward him; José threateningly bars the way.*)
And after you have won the victor's crown,
Earn your sweet reward,
Your señorita's love.
Toreador, your prize is love!
(*His voice fades away in the distance.*)

ACT IV

No 25 CHORUS

(*A square in Seville: at the back, the walls of an ancient amphitheatre; the entrance is closed by a long awning.*)

VENDORS AND PEDDLERS
Get your program for the bullfight!
Just a quarter, just a quarter!
Buy a trinket for the ladies!
Wine and water, wine and water!
Who wants to buy a souvenir?
Cigarettes and cigarros here!
Pretty combs to wear in your hair!
Sweet wine! And beer!
A jug of water!
Toys for the children and balloons!
Coconuts, dates and macaroons!
Colored beads for ladies to wear!
Perfume!
So cheap! At the lowest prices!
Get your program for the bullfight!
Just a quarter, just a quarter!
Ladies and gentlemen!
Señoras and caballeros!

ZUNIGA
I'll take oranges, hurry!

GIRLS
Buy from me Señor, for you and your ladies.

A GIRL (*to Zuniga, who pays her*)
I thank you very much, Señor!

OTHERS (*to Zuniga*)
Buy a shawl, Señor, for the lady!
Who wants to buy a souvenir?
Cigarettes and cigarros here?
Pretty fans to give you some air!
Sweet wine! And beer!
A jug of water!

ZUNIGA
Hey, there! I want two fans!

A MAN (*to Zuniga*)
Will you buy a fine pair of glasses?
Buy a program for the bull fight.

ALL
Buy here from me!

Version II

(*If a ballet is introduced, the following words are sung.*)

Choose your partner,
Take your places for the dancing!
Dance to the ring of tambourines,
To the twang of the mandolins,
Castanets are clicking away,
Come on!
Let's dance!
You Señoritas,
Look for a partner, join the fun,
The fandango and the bolero,
Seguidilla and farandole.
Come on!
Let's dance!
You, Señoritas,
Choose your partner,
Take your places for the dancing!
Ladies and gentlemen,
Señoras and caballeros!
Ev'ryone has happy smiles upon their faces!
We'll dance till it is time to see the Toréros
Take over our places!
Dance to the ring of tambourines . . . etc.
Let's dance till the moment's arrived
To admire the great Toréros.
Take your places for the dancing etc.
Olé! olé!

No. 26 March and Chorus

CHILDREN (*entering*)
The parade, the parade,
Here comes the procession!

CHORUS
Here they come! Yes, here they come!
Yes, here they are.
Here comes the procession!
Look at them, so handsome and
dashing!
We salute the brave Toréros!
In the sun their lances are flashing,
Hurrah, hurrah, hurrah!
Let's give them a rousing welcome,
Toss our hats and wave the sombreros.
We salute the brave Toréros,
Here they come, here they come!
(*The procession begins.*)

CHILDREN
Now it's time for booing and hissing.
There's the sheriff, mean as can be,
No one is as nasty as he.
On holidays he's never missing!
Away, go home, away, go home!

CHORUS
We don't want you here, go home!
Down! Go home, away, go home!
See them march along, proud and
hardy!
Give a cheer for the chulos, too!
Bravo! Bravo!
Hail to the worthy!
Let us cheer the chulos, too!
Oh look, the banderilla men!
See how they swagger in their finery.
Hurrah, hurrah, hurrah!
See there, how proud they are
As they display the lace and sparkling
Gold embroid'ry upon their gala
dress array!
Hello, you banderilla men!

CHILDREN
Another quadrille is approaching!

CHORUS
Another quadrille is approaching!
They are the picadors,
Ah, what handsome men!
So full of pride!
What a thrill to see how their lances
Pierce the raging bull in the side!
The hero! The champion!
Toréro, Toréro!
(*Escamillo enters: beside him Carmen,
radiant with delight and brilliantly
dressed.*)

Escamillo, Escamillo!
Hail Escamillo, hail the Toréro!
Proud as a king, yours is the ring!
One and all, we applaud our hero.
Ev'ryone's looking up to you,
Hail, Escamillo, hail, Escamillo!
Ah! bravo!
Look at him, so handsome and
dashing!
We salute the brave Toréro!
On his sword the sunlight is flashing,
Hurrah, hurrah, hurrah!
Let's give him a rousing welcome,
Toss your caps and wave your
sombrero.
We salute the brave Toréro.
Hail, Escamillo! Ah!
Bravo, bravo, viva, bravo!

ESCAMILLO (*to Carmen*)
If you love me, Carmen,
Then today, of all days,
You will be proud of me,
If you love me, if you love me.

CARMEN
I am yours, Escamillo,
And may God be my witness,
I never loved a man with such passion
before!

BOTH
How I love you, how I love you!

SEVERAL MEN
Back there, back there,
Ev'ryone greet the Mayor!
(*The Mayor appears accompanied by
guards; he enters the amphitheatre
followed by the cuadrilla, the crowd
etc.*)

FRASQUITA
Carmen, do not stay here,
Please follow my advice.

CARMEN
And why, may I ask?

MERCEDES
He is here!

CARMEN
José?

MERCEDES
Yes. Over there, in the crowd he
is hiding.
You can see him.

CARMEN
Yes, I can see him.

FRASQUITA
Be careful!

CARMEN
I am not afraid of a soul in the world.
I will stay, and I'll wait for him here.

MERCEDES
I beg you, believe me, don't stay here!

CARMEN
I'm not afraid!

FRASQUITA
Be careful!
(*The crowd has entered the amphitheatre. Frasquita and Mercedes also
go in. Carmen and José are left
alone.*)

No. 27 Duet and Final Chorus

CARMEN
So you came back?

JOSÉ
I did.

CARMEN
Frasquita and Mercedes both told me
you were near,
That you would look for me.
And they even believe my life will be
in danger.
But I have courage and decided
to stay.

JOSÉ (*gently*)
I do not mean you harm,
I beg you, I implore you.
What used to be is done,
The past is dead, it is over.
Yes, we'll start life anew.
It will be a new existence,
Far away, for me and you.

CARMEN
You are talking like a dreamer.
I won't lie, I won't pretend!
What was between us is over;
Once and for all this is the end!
You know, I never lie,
Once and for all, this is good-bye!

JOSÉ
Carmen, oh let me persuade you,
Yes, life is still before you.
I beg of you, please, come away
with me,
For I adore you.
(*passionately*)
Ah Carmen, come away with me,
We both can be happy still!

CARMEN
No, I have made my decision,
And I know that this is the hour.
But come what may, I do not care,
no, no!
No, I will not give in to you!

JOSÉ
Carmen, life is still before you, etc.

CARMEN
There's no use at all imploring,
My heart holds no love for you.
No, my love for you is dead.
I will not hear what you say.
There's no hope for you.
My love is dead, you hope in vain.
I won't go with you,
Never will!

JOSÉ (*anxiously*)
You don't love me any more?

CARMEN (*tranquilly*)
No, not any more.

JOSÉ
But I, I love you more than ever.
You know, I worship and adore you!

CARMEN
Why do you tell me that?
You waste your words on me!

JOSÉ (*passionately*)
I love you, Carmen, I adore you!
All right, I will remain an outlaw,
I'll rob and steal for you.
I will do anything, yes, all you ask.
If only you will come with me again!
Those golden days, have you forgotten
them?
How much we loved each other!
(*with desperation*)
O Carmen, do not leave me now!

CARMEN
I won't give in, this is good-bye!
Free I was born, and free I shall die!
(*Hearing the cries of the crowd in the
amphitheatre applauding Escamillo,
Carmen makes a gesture of delight.
José keeps his eyes fixed on her.
When Carmen attempts to enter the
amphitheatre José steps in front of
her.*)
CHORUS (*behind scenes*)
Now the fight is getting exciting.
See the bull is raging madly,
Running wildly, he charges forward.
Hurrah, hurrah, hurrah!
Hurrah, it's a marvelous fight!
With lightning speed he charges again!

Escamillo, now show your skill,
Hurrah, hurrah, hurrah!
Toréro!

JOSÉ

Is it he?

CARMEN

Let me go!

JOSÉ

That is your fine new lover
Applauded by the mob!

CARMEN

Let me go, let me go!

JOSÉ

Never, never, you will not run to him!
I swear, I'll make you follow me!

CARMEN

Let me go, Don José, I'll never go
  with you!

JOSÉ

You're on the way to him, Carmen.
(*furiously*) You love this man?

CARMEN

I love him!
And even in the face of death,
With my dying breath,
I shall love him!
(*Carmen again tries to enter the am-
  phitheatre but is stopped by José.*)

CHORUS (*behind scenes*)

Bravo, bravo, this is exciting.
Now the bull is raging madly,
Running wildly, pierced by the lances!
Hurrah, hurrah, hurrah!
This time it's the end of the fight.
The bull is down, he staggers and falls!

JOSÉ (*violently*)

And so I have lost my salvation.
I am damned to hell, so that you
May run to your lover, you harlot,
And in his arms jeer at my despair!
I swear to God you shall not go.
I say, you are coming with me!

CARMEN

No, no, I won't!

JOSÉ

Once again, time is getting short!

CARMEN (*angrily*)

Go ahead, kill me right here,
Or let me go my way!

CHORUS (*behind scenes*)

Escamillo!

DON JOSÉ (*madly*)

For the very last time, answer,
Will you come with me?

CARMEN

No, no! (*tearing a ring from her finger
  and throwing it away*) And here,
  take your ring,
The ring you once gave me!
There!

JOSÉ
(*rushing toward Carmen*)

By God, then die!

CHORUS (*behind scenes*)
(*Carmen attempts to escape, but José
  catches up with her at the entrance
  of the amphitheatre. He stabs her;
  she falls and dies. José, distracted,
  falls on his knees beside her.*)

Toreador, fight well and hard,
Proud as a king,
Yours is the ring.
And after you have won the victor's
  crown,
Earn your sweet reward,
Your señorita's love.
  (*The crowd re-enters the stage.*)
Toreador, your prize is love!

JOSÉ (*in utter despair*)

I have killed my own love!
I killed the one I loved!
She is dead!
O my Carmen, how I loved you!
  (*The curtain falls.*)

WHAT BECAME OF *CARMEN*

Three months to the day after the failure of *Carmen*'s premiere at the Opéra-Comique, Georges Bizet died, never knowing that he had created what more than one critic has called "the perfect opera." Part of the true tragedy of *Carmen* is that the man who made her famous was never aware that both Wagner and Brahms (representing antithetical schools of music) were overjoyed with *Carmen*. Brahms, accompanied on several occasions by Debussy, saw the opera twenty-one times. Sadly, neither did Bizet live to read Tchaikovsky's words: "To me this is in every sense a *chef d'oeuvre,* one of the few pieces that will someday mirror most vividly the musical endeavor of a whole generation. . . . From beginning to end, it is charming and delightful. In it, one finds a number of striking harmonies and entirely new combinations of sound, but these do not exist merely for themselves. Bizet is an artist who pays tribute to modernity, but he is warmed by true inspiration. And what a wonderful subject for an opera! . . . I am convinced that in about ten years *Carmen* will have become the most popular opera in the world."

And it is a tragedy that he was not alive to hear Richard Strauss remark, "If you want to learn how to orchestrate . . . study the score of *Carmen.* What wonderful economy, and how every note rests in its proper place."

Even Friedrich Nietzsche's slightly overblown phrase, motivated in part by his wrath toward his former idol Wagner, would probably have fallen with some satisfaction on Bizet's ears: "And really, I have appeared to myself, every time I have heard *Carmen,* to be more of a philosopher, a better philosopher than at other times: I have become so patient, so happy, so Indian, so sedate. . . . Five hours sitting: the first state of holiness! . . . This music seems to me to be perfect. It approaches lightly, nimbly, and with courtesy. It is amiable, it does not produce *sweat.* 'What is good is easy; everything divine runs with light feet':—the first proposition of my aesthetics. This music is wicked, subtle, and fatalistic; it remains popular at the same time. . . . It is rich. It is precise. It builds, it organizes, it completes; it is thus the antithesis to the polypus in music, 'infinite melody.'"

So much for criticism and the intellectuals—what about the audiences? How did they receive *Carmen* after her initial failure? Ellen Bieler tells us:

"In the fall of 1875, *Carmen* was a success in Vienna, and the next year in Brussels. . . . *Carmen* came to the United States in 1878, when Colonel James Mapleson's troupe presented it at the New York Academy of Music. Two days later, a rival company put it on in Philadelphia, and a battle soon arose between the two productions, with Mapleson claiming that the other was not the real *Carmen* but only a shoddy, feeble expansion of the piano score. Both troupes eventually toured the country with *Carmen* in their repertoires. In New York the opera was misunderstood by both audience and critics, but it soon became popular overnight, and led all other operas in number of performances.

"By now the Parisian audiences began to clamor for a revival of the opera, and in 1883 *Carmen* was again presented, but in a production that suggests that the director hoped once and for all to get rid of the opera by sabotaging it. The music was slowed down; the chorus returned to the statuesque poses Bizet had fought; Lillas Pastia's low tavern became a respectable hotel in which beautifully dressed guests sat while a classical ballet paced. Don José and Escamillo discussed their differences amicably instead of fighting with knives. Carmen was amiable and chic, and José managed to drop his dagger when about to stab her. The critical response was a shout of 'Desecration.' Finally, the management had to re-establish the true *Carmen*. Since then it has been a mainstay of the Opéra-Comique, its thousandth performance having occurred in 1904. By 1938, the hundredth anniversary of Bizet's birth, *Carmen* had been performed at the Opéra-Comique 2,271 times."

Carmen's popularity, however, has not been limited to the opera stage. Billy Rose produced and Oscar Hammerstein II wrote one of the most successful of Broadway shows, using Bizet's music and new lyrics for *Carmen Jones,* which later became a tremendously popular motion picture. On the screen *Carmen* has been represented more than any other heroine from fiction. Thirty-eight films, four in the past two years, have been inspired by her. Chaplin, de Mille, Vidor, Preminger, Saura, Zeffirelli, Godard, and Rosi are a few of the directors who have guided actresses from Theda Bara to Rita Hayworth through the role. Unquestionably the most exciting Carmen film is the Saura-Gades dance version which, like Mérimée's novel, is a story within a story.

Of the interpretations of Carmen in my experience, the most moving was not in an opera or even in a film, but in a ballet. My favorite Carmen was danced by Alicia Alonso, then over sixty years old and nearly blind, with her Cuban National Ballet in the Lope de Vega Theatre directly across the street from the old tobacco factory in Sevilla. The opera in its entirety I first saw in Rome, shortly before I moved to Sevilla in 1959, and of that performance I can't recall who was more animated, the singers on stage or the audience who protested their performances.

Of all the performances of *Carmen,* however, the most meaningful to me was the one mentioned by James Michener, staged fifteen years or more ago in the Sevilla bullring in which, under a full moon, Antonio Gades (who also performed in the Saura film) danced amid hundreds of extras, prancing horses, and strutting toreros on the golden sand of the Maestranza not more than fifty feet from where Bizet's gypsy girl had been stabbed to death by her soldier lover. The night was charged with emotion as *Carmen* came full circle. More than a hundred years later, she had returned to the Sevilla which had given birth to her, after captivating and seducing not only Don José—but the entire world.

Sevilla is *Carmen* and *Carmen* is Sevilla. That is the way it was and how I hope it will always be.